World Geography Questionnaires

United States of America

Volume VII

Kenneth Ma & Jennifer Fu

Geography Collections

Write to geopublish@gmail.com for more information about this book.

Book Title: World Geography Questionnaires
              United States of America
              Volume VII
Author: Kenneth Ma & Jennifer Fu
ISBN-10:   1477408673
ISBN-13:   978-1477408674

Table of Contents

Introduction 1
United States of America 2
Alabama 4
Alaska 7
Arizona 11
Arkansas 14
California 17
Colorado 21
Connecticut 25
Delaware 28
District of Columbia 30
Florida 32
Georgia 36
Hawaii 39
Idaho 42
Illinois 45
Indiana 48
Iowa 50
Kansas 53
Kentucky 55
Louisiana 58
Maine 62
Maryland 65
Massachusetts 69
Michigan 73
Minnesota 77
Mississippi 80
Missouri 84
Montana 87
Nebraska 90
Nevada 93
New Hampshire 96
New Jersey 100
New Mexico 103
New York 107
North Carolina 111
North Dakota 115
Ohio 118
Oklahoma 121
Oregon 125
Pennsylvania 128
Rhode Island 131

South Carolina 134

South Dakota 137

Tennessee 140

Texas 143

Utah 147

Vermont 150

Virginia 153

Washington 156

West Virginia 159

Wisconsin 162

Wyoming 165

Miscellaneous 169

Bibliography 172

Other Books 173

About the Authors 174

Introduction

As a young child, I always enjoyed looking at maps to better understand the world around me. When I heard of the National Geography Bee, I finally got a chance to put it into use. During the contest, I realized how there wasn't just one study guide that covered the entire world effectively. After the contest was over, I thought that the people who had to compete after me shouldn't have to go through the same pain studying from tons of different study guides as well as helping those who simply want to learn more about the world. This got me started on this series of books.

This is the seventh book of the World Geography Questionnaires series, consisting of six books which ask questions on a different region of the world and a book defining geography terms. With the exception of the sixth book, each book describes important facts about each country (states in this book) in that region in a question and answer format. This book covers the United States of America.

As more books are published, a lot of improvements are made based on the feedback. If you have any questions or comments, please send an email to geopublish@gmail.com.

This book would have never been possible without the help of my parents, especially my mom, who is also my co-author, my teachers, and my sister. Many thanks to my parents for encouraging me and pushing me to go on, my teacher, Mr. Blair, for starting and widening my interest for geography, and my sister, Hermione, who helped me find the information and get to know it better.

Kenneth Ma

United States of America

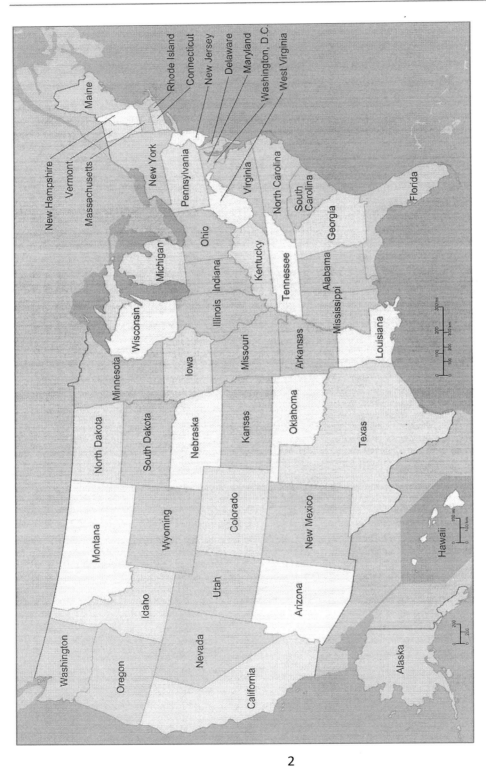

The United States of America (also called the United States, the U.S., the USA, America, and the States) is a federal constitutional republic comprising 50 states and a federal district.

The 48 contiguous states of the United States of America are located in the northern hemisphere and almost totally in the western hemisphere. It is bordered on the north by Canada, on the east by Atlantic Ocean, on the south by Mexico on the southeast by the Gulf of Mexico, and on the west by the Pacific Ocean. Alaska is northwest of mainland United States, bordered by Canada to the east, the Pacific Ocean to the west and south, and the Arctic Ocean to the north. Hawaii is southwest of mainland United States, surrounded entirely by the Pacific Ocean.

The 48 contiguous states of the United States have the Rocky Mountains and Cascade Ranges in the west, and the Appalachian Mountains in the east. Central United States is dominated by the Great Plains, which run through North Dakota down to Texas. The Missouri-Mississippi river system, the longest river in the United States of America, is the 4th longest river in the world. The river system has its source in Lake Itasca in Minnesota, and its mouth in the Gulf of Mexico in Louisiana. The Great Lakes are a chain of freshwater lakes located in eastern North America, on the Canada-United States border. The Great Lakes consist of Lakes Superior, Michigan, Huron, Erie, and Ontario. These lakes form the largest group of freshwater lakes on Earth.

The United States also own these territories: American Samoa, Baker Island, Guam, Howland Island, Jarvis Island, Johnston Atoll, Kingman Reef, Midway Islands, Navassa Island, Northern Mariana Islands, Palmyra Atoll, Puerto Rico, Virgin Islands, and Wake Island.

The northernmost point in all United States territory is Point Barrow in Alaska. The southernmost point in all United States territory is Rose Atoll in the American Samoa. The southernmost point in the 50 states is Ka Lae in Hawaii. The southernmost point in the 48 contiguous states is Western Dry Rocks in Florida. The easternmost point in all United States territory is Pochnoi Point in Alaska. The easternmost point in the 48 contiguous states is West Quoddy Head in Maine. The westernmost point in all United States territory is Amatignak Island in Alaska. The westernmost point in the 48 contiguous states is Umatilla Reef in Washington. The geographic center of all 50 states is approximately 20 miles (34 km) north of Belle Fourche, South Dakota. The geographic center of the 48 contiguous states is approximately 4 miles (6 km) west of Lebanon, Kansas.

Alabama

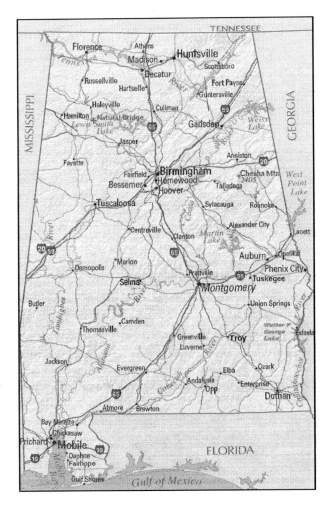

1. Which state borders Alabama in the north?
   Tennessee
2. Which state borders Alabama in the east?
   Georgia
3. Which state borders Alabama in the south?
   Florida
4. Which state borders Alabama in the west?
   Mississippi
5. Which river makes up part of the eastern boundary of Alabama?
   Chattahoochee River
6. Which water body lies to the south of Alabama?
   Gulf of Mexico
7. What are the nicknames of Alabama?

Yellowhammer State; Heart of Dixie; Cotton State

8. What is the state motto of Alabama?
   We Dare to Defend Our Rights

9. What is the state song of Alabama?
   Alabama

10. What is the state tree of Alabama?
    Longleaf Pine

11. What is the state flower of Alabama?
    Camellia

12. What is the state wildflower of Alabama?
    Oak-leaf Hydrangea

13. What is the state nut of Alabama?
    Pecan

14. What is the state bird of Alabama?
    Yellowhammer

15. What is the state game bird of Alabama?
    Wild Turkey

16. What is the state horse of Alabama?
    Racking Horse

17. What is the state insect of Alabama?
    Monarch Butterfly

18. What is the state butterfly and state mascot of Alabama?
    Eastern Tiger Swallowtail

19. What is the state saltwater fish of Alabama?
    (Fighting) Tarpon

20. What is the state freshwater fish of Alabama?
    Largemouth Bass

21. What is the state amphibian of Alabama?
    Red Hills Salamander

22. What is the state shell of Alabama?
    Scaphella Junonia Johnstoneae

23. What is the state fossil of Alabama?
    Basilosaurus Cetoides (an extinct whale)

24. What is the state rock of Alabama?
    Marble

25. What is the state gemstone of Alabama?
    Star Blue Quartz

26. What is the state mineral of Alabama?
    Hematite (Red iron ore)

27. What is the state soil of Alabama?
    Bama Soil Series

28. What is the state dance of Alabama?
    Folk Dance

29. What is the state quilt of Alabama?
    Pine Burr Quilt

30. What is the capital of Alabama?
Montgomery
31. What is the largest city by population in Alabama?
Birmingham
32. What is the largest city by area in Alabama?
Huntsville
33. Who explored Mobile Bay in 1519?
Alonzo Alvarez de Piñeda (Spanish explorer)
34. Who explored Alabama in 1539?
Hernando de Soto (Spanish explorer)
35. The first capital of French Louisiana was built in which city of Alabama in 1712?
Mobile
36. In which year did Britain control Alabama after the decisive victory of the French and Indian War?
1763
37. When was the Territory of Mississippi organized from western Georgia, including Alabama?
April 7th, 1798
38. When was the Territory of Alabama established?
August 15th, 1817
39. When was Alabama admitted to the Union?
December 14th, 1819 (22nd)
40. During which period did Alabama secede from the Union?
1861 – 1868
41. In which city of Alabama did the Montgomery Bus Boycott start in 1955, led by Martin Luther King Jr.?
Montgomery
42. What is the area of Alabama?
52,419 sq mi / 135,765 km^2 (30th)
43. What is the population of Alabama?
4,849,377 (by 2014)
44. What is the topography of Alabama?
Cumberland Plateau and Appalachian Mountains in the northeast; Piedmont Plateau in the central east; Gulf Coastal Plain in the south
45. What is the highest point of Alabama, located in the Appalachian Mountains?
Mount Cheaha (2,413 ft / 735 m)
46. What is the lowest point of Alabama?
Gulf of Mexico (0 ft / 0 m)
47. How long is the coastline of Alabama?
53 mi / 85 km (18th)
48. What are the major rivers in Alabama?
Tombigbee River, Alabama River, Tennessee River, and Chattahoochee River
49. What are the major lakes in Alabama?
Guntersville Lake, Wilson Lake, West Point Lake, and Lewis Smith Lake
50. What is the climate in Alabama?
Humid subtropical

51. What are the natural resources in Alabama?
    Wide variety of soils, coal, iron ore, limestone, bauxite, white marble, and timber
52. What are the natural hazards in Alabama?
    Hurricanes and tropical storms
53. What are the major industries in Alabama?
    Agriculture hydroelectric power, mining, and steel-making

Alaska

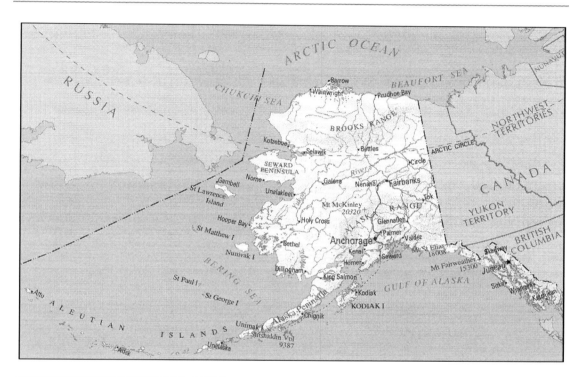

54. Which country borders Alaska to the east?
    Canada
55. Which water body lies to the south of Alaska?
    Pacific Ocean
56. Which water body lies to the west of Alaska?
    Bering Strait

57. Which country lies to the west of Alaska, across the Bering Strait?
Russia
58. Which water body lies to the north of Alaska?
Arctic Ocean
59. What is the nickname of Alaska?
Last Frontier
60. What is the state motto of Alaska?
North to the Future
61. What is the state song of Alaska?
Alaska's Flag
62. What is the state tree of Alaska?
Sitka Spruce
63. What is the state flower of Alaska?
Forget Me Not
64. What is the state bird of Alaska?
Willow Ptarmigan
65. What is the state land mammal of Alaska?
Moose
66. What is the state marine mammal of Alaska?
Bowhead Whale
67. What is the state fish of Alaska?
King Salmon
68. What is the state insect of Alaska?
Four-spot Skimmer Dragonfly
69. What is the state fossil of Alaska?
Woolly Mammoth
70. What is the state mineral of Alaska?
Gold
71. What is the state gem of Alaska?
Jade
72. What is the state sport of Alaska?
Dog Mushing
73. What is the capital of Alaska?
Juneau
74. What is the largest city by population in Alaska?
Anchorage
75. What is the largest city by area in the United States, located in Alaska?
Yakutat
76. Who explored Alaska in 1741?
Vitus Jonassen Bering (Danish navigator in the service of the Russian Navy)
77. During the 18th century, which countries explored Alaska besides Russia?
Spain and Britain
78. Which city became the first European (Russian) settlement in Alaska, established in 1763?
Kodiak
79. During which period did the Russian America, Russian colonial possessions at the present-

day Alaska and parts of California and Hawaii, exist?
1799 – 1867

80. When did Alaska officially become the property of the United States after being purchased from the Russian Empire for $7.2 million (2 cents per acre or 5 cents per hectare)?
October 18th, 1867

81. In the 1890s, which gold rush brought thousands of miners and settlers to Alaska after Joe Juneau's discovery of gold in 1880?
Klondike Gold Rush (also called Yukon Gold Rush)

82. When was the Territory of Alaska established?
August 24th, 1912

83. Which war was started in 1942 when Japan invaded Aleutian Islands?
One Thousand Mile War (the first battle fought on American soil since the Civil War)

84. When was Alaska admitted to the Union?
January 3rd, 1959 (49th)

85. How many people were killed by the 9.2 magnitude Alaska earthquake (also called the Great Alaskan Earthquake, the Portage Earthquake or the Good Friday Earthquake) on March 27th, 1964?
130

86. The discovery of oil in 1968 at Prudhoe Bay and the 1977 completion of the Trans-Alaska Pipeline led to what kind of boom in Alaska?
Oil boom

87. In 1989, which oil tanker hit a reef in the Prince William Sound, spilling between 11 and 35 million gallons (42,000 and 130,000 m³) of crude oil over 1,100 miles (1,600 km) of coastline?
Exxon Valdez

88. What is the area of Alaska?
663,268 sq mi / 1,717,854 km^2 (1st)

89. Which county in Alaska is the largest county by area in the United States?
Unorganized Borough (323,440 sq mi / 837,710 km^2)

90. How many of the largest counties by area in the United States are located in Alaska?
5

91. What is the population of Alaska?
736,732 (by 2014)

92. What is the topography of Alaska?
Brooks Range in the north; Alaska Range in the central south; Aleutian Range in the southwest; Aleutian Islands in the further southwest; Alexandra Archipelago in the southeast

93. What is the North America's highest point, located in the Alaska Range?
Mount McKinley (20,320 ft / 6,194 m)

94. How many peaks are located in Alaska among the 20 highest peaks in the United States?
17

95. What is the lowest point of Alaska?
Pacific Ocean (0 ft / 0 m)

96. How long is the coastline of Alaska?
6,640 mi / 10,686 km (1st)

97. What are the major rivers in Alaska, among 12,000 rivers (9,728 officially named)?
   Yukon River, Kuskokwim River, Colville River, and Copper River
98. What are the major lakes in Alaska, among 3,000,000 lakes (3,197 officially named natural lakes and 67 officially named reservoirs)?
   Iliamna Lake, Aleknagik Lake, Becharof Lake, and Clark Lake
99. Which national parks are located in Alaska?
   Denali National Park (9,492 sq mi / 24,585 km²), Gates Of The Arctic National Park (13,238 sq mi / 39,460 km²), Glacier Bay National Park (5,130 sq mi / 13,287 km²), Katmai National Park (7,383 sq mi / 19,120 km²), Kenai Fjords National Park (1,760 sq mi / 4,600 km²), Kobuk Valley National Park (2,609 sq mi / 6,757 km²), Lake Clark National Park (4,093 sq mi / 10,602 km²), and Wrangell - Saint Elias National Park and Preserve (20,587 sq mi / 53,321 km²)
100. What is the Denali National Park famous for?
   Mount McKinley, as well as other spectacular mountains and many large glaciers
101. What is the Gates of the Arctic National Park famous for?
   Untouched wilderness above the Arctic Circle, glacier valleys, rugged mountains, and miles of arctic tundra
102. What is the Glacier Bay National Park famous for?
   Snow-capped mountain ranges rising to over 15,000 ft (4,572 m), coastal beaches with protected coves, deep fjords, tidewater glaciers, coastal and estuarine waters, freshwater lakes, and a wide variety of seabirds, marine and land mammals
103. What is the Katmai National Park famous for?
   Mount Katmai; Valley of Ten Thousand Smokes, a massive 40 mi (64 km) long pyroclastic ash flow created by the spectacular eruption of Novarupta Volcano in 1912; 14 active volcanoes; the world's largest protected brown bear population
104. What is the Kenai Fjords National Park famous for?
   An abundant array of tidewater and piedmont glaciers within the crystal green waters of the Fjords; marine wildlife includes otters, sea lions, harbor seals, humpback and orca whales, porpoises, puffins and kittiwakes
105. What is the Kobuk Valley National Park famous for?
   Baird Mountains in the north; Kobuk Sand Dunes in the south; Kobuk River Valley in between
106. What is the Lake Clark National Park famous for?
   Rugged mountains from three ranges, two active volcanoes, and many lakes and streams; salmon fisheries; abundant wildlife; traditional lifestyles of local residents
107. What is the Wrangell - Saint Elias National Park and Preserve famous for?
   The largest in the United States; Bagley Icefield; Hubbard, Nabesna and Malaspina Glaciers; Mountain Wrangell and Mount Saint Elias, and the convergence of four major mountain ranges; Abandoned Kennicott copper mine
108. Which national forest in Alaska is the largest in the United States?
   Tongass National Forest (27,000 sq mi / 69,000 km²)
109. Which settlement in Alaska has the country's lowest recorded temperature of -80 °F (-62 °C) in January 1971?
   Prospect Creek
110. What is the climate in Alaska?

An exceptionally variable and unpredictable climate; mid-latitude oceanic climate and subarctic oceanic climate in the southeast; subarctic climate in the central south and interior; arctic climate in the extreme north

111. What are the natural resources in Alaska?
Crude oil, natural gas, timber, and fish

112. What are the natural hazards in Alaska?
Earthquakes, hurricanes, wildfires, floods, and active volcanoes

113. What are the major industries in Alaska?
Petroleum

Arizona

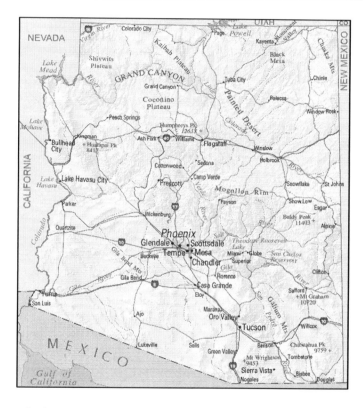
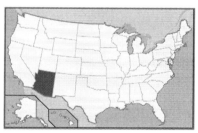

114. Which state borders Arizona in the north?
Utah

115. Which state borders Arizona in the east?
New Mexico

116. Which states border Arizona in the west?
California and Nevada

117. Which state touches Arizona in the northeast?
Colorado

118. Which country borders Arizona in the south?
Mexico

119. Which river makes up most of the western boundary of Arizona?
Colorado River
120. What are the nicknames of Arizona?
Grand Canyon State; Copper State
121. What is the state motto of Arizona?
God Enriches
122. What is the state song of Arizona?
Arizona
123. What is the state tree of Arizona?
Yellow Palo Verde
124. What is the state flower of Arizona?
Saguaro Cactus Blossom
125. What is the state bird of Arizona?
Cactus Wren
126. What is the state mammal of Arizona?
Ringtail
127. What is the state reptile of Arizona?
Arizona Ridgenose Rattlesnake
128. What is the state amphibian of Arizona?
Arizona Tree Frog
129. What is the state fish of Arizona?
Arizona Trout
130. What is the state insect of Arizona?
Two-tailed Swallowtail
131. What is the state fossil of Arizona?
Petrified Wood
132. What is the state gemstone of Arizona?
Turquoise
133. What is the state necktie of Arizona?
Bolo Tie
134. What are the state colors of Arizona?
Blue and Gold
135. What is the capital of Arizona?
Phoenix (the largest city by population and area)
136. Who explored Arizona in 1539?
Marcos de Niza (Spanish Franciscan)
137. In which year was Tucson founded as a Spanish military garrison?
1775
138. In which year did Arizona become part of Mexico from Spain?
1821
139. By which treaty was most of Arizona (north of the Gila River) granted to the United States in 1848?
Treaty of Guadalupe Hidalgo
140. When did the Gadsden Purchase acquire the southern Arizona to the United States?
December 30th, 1853

141. When was Arizona separated from the Territory of New Mexico to become the Territory of Arizona?
February 24th, 1863
142. When was Arizona admitted to the Union?
February 14th, 1912 (48th)
143. Which city in Arizona, located in Tombstone Canyon, is known as the Queen of the Copper Mines?
Bisbee
144. What is the area of Arizona?
113,998 sq mi / 295,254 km^2 (6th)
145. What is the population of Arizona?
6,731,484 (by 2014)
146. What is the topography of Arizona?
Cumberland Plateau in the north; Grand Canyon in the northwest; Painted Desert in the central north; Mogollon Rim in the center; Sonoran Desert in the southwest; 193 mountain ranges
147. What is the highest point of Arizona, also the highest of the San Francisco Peaks - a group of extinct volcanic peaks?
Humphreys Peak (12,633 ft / 3,851 m)
148. What is the lowest point of Arizona?
Colorado River (70 ft / 22 m)
149. What are the major rivers in Arizona?
Colorado River, Little Colorado River, and Gila River
150. What are the major lakes in Arizona?
Lake Mead, Lake Havasu, and Roosevelt Lake
151. Which national parks are located in Arizona?
Grand Canyon National Park (1,902 sq mi / 4,927 km^2), Petrified Forest National Park (146 sq mi/ 380 km^2), and Saguaro National Park (142 sq mi/ 370 km^2)
152. What is the Grand Canyon National Park famous for?
The 277 mi (446 km) long, up to 1 mi (1.6 km) deep, and up to 15 mi (24 km) wide canyon, with colorful layers of the Colorado Plateau in mesas and canyon walls
153. What is the Petrified Forest National Park famous for?
A great concentration of 225-million-year-old petrified wood, surrounded by the Painted Desert
154. What is the Saguaro National Park famous for?
Saguaro Cactus in the Sonoran Desert
155. Which part of Arizona observes the daylight savings time change?
Navajo Nation
156. What is the Navajo Nation?
A semi-autonomous Native American-governed territory covering 27,425 sq mi (71,000 km^2), occupying all of northeastern Arizona, the southeastern portion of Utah, and northwestern New Mexico
157. What is the capital of the Navajo Nation, located in Arizona?
Window Rock
158. What was the oldest Native American settlement in the United States, located in Arizona?

Oraibi (established before 1100 AD)

159. The original London Bridge was shipped stone-by-stone and reconstructed in which city, located in Arizona?
Lake Havasu City

160. Which city in Arizona is the driest city in the United States, measured by the average annual precipitation in inches and number of days per year with rain?
Yuma

161. What is the climate in Arizona?
Arid or semi-arid

162. What are the natural resources in Arizona?
Warm climate, copper, coal, gold, petroleum, pumice, silver, stone, and uranium

163. What are the natural hazards in Arizona?
Earthquakes, hurricanes, and wildfires

164. What are the major industries in Arizona?
Mining, manufacturing, and tourism

Arkansas

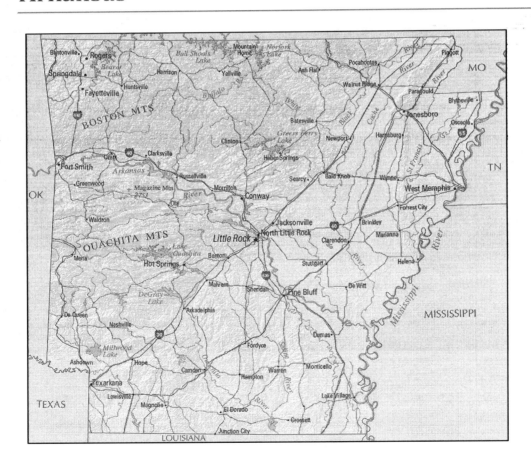

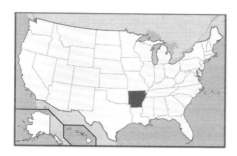

165. Which state borders Arkansas in the north and northeast?
   Missouri
166. Which states border Arkansas in the east?
   Tennessee and Mississippi
167. Which state borders Arkansas in the southwest?
   Texas
168. Which state borders Arkansas in the south?
   Louisiana
169. Which state borders Arkansas in the west?
   Oklahoma
170. Which river makes up the eastern border of Arkansas?
   Mississippi River
171. What are the nicknames of Arkansas?
   Natural State; Land of Opportunity
172. What is the state motto of Arkansas?
   The People Rule
173. What are the state songs of Arkansas?
   Arkansas; Oh, Arkansas
174. What is the state tree of Arkansas?
   Loblolly Pine
175. What is the state flower of Arkansas?
   Apple Blossom
176. What is the state bird of Arkansas?
   Mockingbird
177. What is the state fruit and blossom of Arkansas?
   South Arkansas Vine Ripe Pink Tomato
178. What is the state mammal of Arkansas?
   White-tailed Deer
179. What is the state insect of Arkansas?
   Honeybee
180. What is the state mineral of Arkansas?
   Bauxite
181. What is the state gem of Arkansas?
   Diamond
182. What is the state rock of Arkansas?
   Quartz Crystal

183. What is the state beverage of Arkansas?
    Milk
184. What is the state instrument of Arkansas?
    Fiddle
185. What is the state dance of Arkansas?
    Square Dance
186. What is the capital of Arkansas?
    Little Rock (the largest city by population and area)
187. Who explored Arkansas in 1541?
    Hernando de Soto (Spanish explorer)
188. What was the first European (French) settlement in Arkansas, founded in 1686?
    Arkansas Post
189. In which year was Georgetown, the oldest permanent settlement in Arkansas, established?
    1789
190. Arkansas was purchased from France by which treaty signed on April 30th, 1803?
    Louisiana Purchase
191. When was the Territory of Missouri, including Arkansas, established?
    June 4th, 1812
192. When was the Territory of Arkansas split from the Territory of Missouri?
    July 4th, 1819
193. When was Arkansas admitted to the Union?
    June 15th, 1836 (25th)
194. During which period did Arkansas secede from the Union?
    1861 – 1865
195. What is the area of Arkansas?
    53,179 sq mi / 137,733 km^2 (29th)
196. What is the population of Arkansas?
    2,966,369 (by 2014)
197. What is the topography of Arkansas?
    Crowley's Ridge in the east; Ozark Plateau including the Ozark Mountains in the northwest;
    Ouachita Mountains in the central west; the southern and eastern parts of Arkansas are
    called the Lowlands
198. What is the highest point of Arkansas, located in the Ouachita Mountains?
    Mount Magazine (2,753 ft / 840 m)
199. What is the lowest point of Arkansas?
    Ouachita River (55 ft / 17 m)
200. What are the major rivers in Arkansas?
    Arkansas River and Mississippi River
201. What are the major lakes in Arkansas?
    Lake Ouachita and Bull Shoals Lake
202. The Arkansas Post Canal, part of the McClellan-Kerr Arkansas River Navigation System,
    connects which two rivers?
    Arkansas River and White River
203. Which national park is located in Arkansas?
    Hot Springs National Park (9 sq mi / 22 km^2)

204. What is the Hot Springs National Park, the smallest national park in the United States, famous for?

47 gushing springs that produces millions of gallons of hot water

205. Which city in Arkansas is known as the Quartz Crystal Capital of the World?

Mount Ida

206. Which city in Arkansas claims to be the Spinach Capital of the World?

Alma

207. What is the climate in Arkansas?

Humid tropical

208. What are the natural resources in Arkansas?

Soil, oil, coal, bauxite, trees, and rice

209. What are the natural hazards in Arkansas?

Earthquakes, hurricanes, and tornados

210. What are the major industries in Arkansas?

Agriculture, paper and wood products, electronic equipment, and mining

California

211. Which state borders California in the north?

Oregon

212. Which states border California in the east?

Nevada and Arizona

213. Which country borders California in the south?

Mexico

214. Which river makes up part of the eastern boundary of California?

Colorado River

215. Which water body lies to the west of California?

Pacific Ocean

216. What is the nickname of California?

Golden State

217. What is the state motto of California?

Eureka

218. What is the state song of California?

I Love You, California

219. What is the state tree of California?

Redwood

220. What is the state flower of California?

California Poppy

221. What is the state grass of California?

Purple Needlegrass

222. What is the state bird of California?

California Valley Quail

223. What is the state mammal of California?

California Grizzly Bear

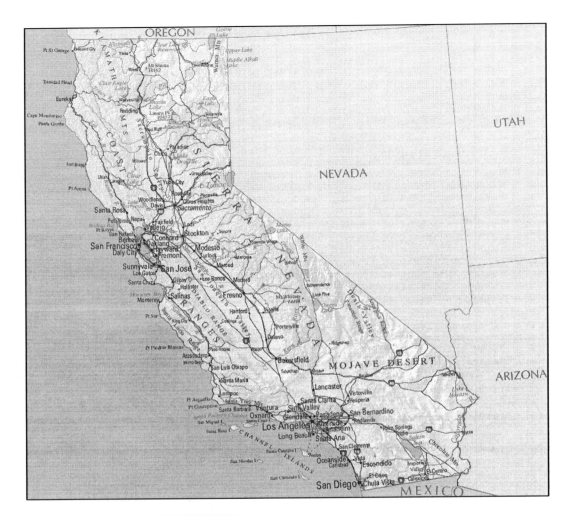

224. What is the state marine mammal of California?
     Gray Whale
225. What is the state reptile of California?
     Desert Tortoise
226. What is the state insect of California?
     California Dogface Butterfly
227. What is the state fish of California?
     Golden Trout

228. What is the state marine fish of California?
Garibaldi
229. What is the state fossil of California?
Smilodon Fatalis (Saber-tooth Tiger)
230. What is the state rock of California?
Serpentinite
231. What is the state mineral of California?
Gold
232. What is the state gem of California?
Benitoite
233. What is the capital of California?
Sacramento
234. What is the largest city by population and area in California?
Los Angeles
235. Who explored California in 1542?
Juan Rodriguez Cabrillo (Portuguese explorer)
236. In which year did California become part of Alta California that was a province and territory in the Viceroyalty of New Spain and later a territory and department in Mexico?
1769
237. The Presidio and Mission of which city, founded in 1769, was the first European (Spanish) settlement in California?
San Diego
238. By which treaty was California granted to the United States in 1848?
Treaty of Guadalupe Hidalgo
239. How did the California Gold Rush (1848–1855) begin?
James W. Marshall found gold at Sutter's Mill, in Coloma, California on January 24th, 1848
240. Who were the forty-niners?
Prospectors and other settlers that came for the California Gold Rush in 1849
241. When did Sacramento become the oldest incorporated city in California?
February 27th, 1850
242. In the late 1850s, the Kennedy Mine, located in which city of California, served as one of the richest gold mines in the world and the deepest mine in North America?
Jackson
243. When was California admitted to the Union?
September 9th, 1850 (31st)
244. What was the first motion picture theater opened in Los Angeles on April 2nd, 1902?
Electric Theatre
245. What is the capital of the Silicon Valley, home to many of the world's largest technology corporations?
San Jose
246. Which city in California is known as the Avocado Capital of the World and hosts an annual Avocado Festival?
Fallbrook
247. Which city in California is known as the Artichoke Capital of the World?
Castroville

248. Which city in California proclaims itself the Raisin Capital of the World?
Fresno
249. What is the area of California?
163,696 sq mi / 423,970 km^2 (3rd)
250. Which county in California is the largest county by area in the 48 contiguous United States?
San Bernardino County (20,105 sq mi / 52,072 km^2)
251. Which bay in California is considered the world's largest landlocked harbor?
San Francisco Bay
252. What is the population of California?
38,802,500 (by 2014)
253. What is California's rank by economy among the 50 states?
1st
254. What is the topography of California?
Cascade Range and Sierra Nevada Mountains in the east; Central Valley in the center; Coastal Range in the west; Mojave Desert and Sonoran Desert in the southeast
255. What is the highest point of California, located in the Sierra Nevada Mountains?
Mount Whitney (14,495 ft / 4,418 m)
256. What is the Mount Whitney's rank by height in the contiguous United States?
1st
257. What is the lowest point of California, located in the Mojave Desert?
Badwater Basin in Death Valley (-282 ft / -86m)
258. What is the northern half of the Central Valley called?
Sacramento Valley
259. What is the southern half of the Central Valley called?
San Joaquin Valley
260. How long is the coastline of California?
840 mi / 1,352 km (3rd)
261. What are the major rivers in California?
Sacramento River, Colorado River and the San Joaquin River
262. What are the major lakes in California?
Salton Sea, Lake Tahoe, and Shasta Lake
263. Which national parks are located in California?
Channel Islands National Park (390 sq mi / 1,010 km^2), Death Valley National Park (in California and Nevada, 5,262 sq mi / 13,629 km^2), Joshua Tree National Park (1,234 sq mi / 3,196 km^2), Lassen National Park (166 sq mi / 431 km^2), Pinnacle National Park (5 sq mi/ 8 km^2), Redwood National Park (176 sq mi / 455 km^2), Sequoia National Park (631 sq mi / 1,635 km^2), Kings Canyon National Park (722 sq mi / 1,869 km^2), and Yosemite National Park (1,189 sq mi / 3,081 km^2)
264. What is the Channel Islands National Park famous for?
Over 2,000 species of land plants and animals, 145 unique to the islands
265. What is the Death Valley National Park famous for?
It is the lowest, driest, and hottest place in the North America, which has canyons, colorful badlands, sand dunes, mountains, and over 1000 species of plants in this graben on a fault line
266. What was the Death Valley's recorded the country's highest temperature on July 10th,

1913?
134 °F (57 °C)
267. What is the Joshua Tree National Park famous for?
Joshua trees, the bizarre trees that dot the landscape; sand dunes, dry lakes, rugged mountains, and granite monoliths
268. What is the Lassen National Park famous for?
Lassen Peak, the largest plug dome volcano in the world; hydrothermal areas, including fumaroles, boiling pools, and steaming ground, heated by molten rock under the peak
269. What is the Redwood National Park famous for?
Almost half of all remaining Coastal Redwoods, the tallest trees on Earth; coastline with tide pools and seastacks
270. What is the Sequoia National Park famous for?
Giant Sequoias, including the world's largest tree, General Sherman; over 240 caves; Mount Whitney; the granite dome Moro Rock
271. What is the Kings Canyon National Park famous for?
Giant sequoia, including the world's 2nd largest tree, General Grant Tree; Kings River; the granite Kings Canyon
272. What is the Yosemite National Park famous for?
Half Dome and El Capitan rising from the central glacier-formed Yosemite Valley; Yosemite Falls, North America's tallest waterfall; Three Giant Sequoia groves
273. The Inyo National Forest is home to what kind of tree that is considered the oldest living species, with some over 4,600 years old?
Bristle Cone Pine
274. Approximately how many detectable seismic tremors are there in California annually?
500,000
275. What is the climate in California?
From arid to subarctic; some coastal areas have Mediterranean climate, with somewhat rainy winters and dry summers
276. What are the natural resources in California?
Soil, climate, oil, timber, coal, and water
277. What are the natural hazards in California?
Tsunamis, floods, droughts, Santa Ana winds, wildfires, landslides, volcanoes, and earthquakes
278. What are the major industries in California?
Agriculture oil, mining, electronics, movie making/entertainment, and tourism

Colorado

279. Which state borders Colorado in the northeast?
Nebraska
280. Which state borders Colorado in the north?
Wyoming
281. Which state borders Colorado in the east?
Kansas

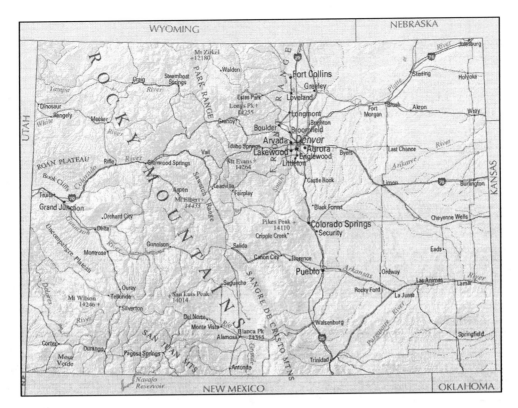

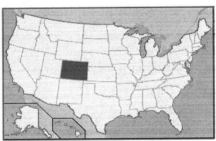

282. Which state borders Colorado in the west?
    Utah

283. Which states border Colorado in the south?
    New Mexico and Oklahoma

284. Which state touches Colorado in the southwest?
    Arizona

285. What is the nickname of Colorado?
    Centennial State

286. What is the state motto of Colorado?
    Nothing Without Providence

287. What is the state song of Colorado?
    Where the Columbines Grow

288. What is the state tree of Colorado?

Colorado Blue Spruce
289. What is the state flower of?
Rocky Mountain Columbine
290. What is the state grass of Colorado?
Blue Grama Grass
291. What is the state bird of Colorado?
Lark Bunting
292. What is the state animal of Colorado?
Rocky Mountain Bighorn Sheep
293. What is the state insect of Colorado?
Colorado Hairstreak Butterfly
294. What is the state fish of Colorado?
Greenback Cutthroat Trout
295. What is the state fossil of Colorado?
Stegosaurus
296. What is the state gemstone of Colorado?
Aquamarine
297. What is the state soil of Colorado?
Seitz
298. What is the state dance of Colorado?
Square Dance
299. What is the capital of Colorado?
Denver (the largest city by population)
300. What is the largest city by area in Colorado?
Colorado Springs
301. Who explored Colorado in 1598?
Juan de Oñate (Spanish explorer)
302. Who claimed the Territory of Colorado in 1706?
Juan Ulibarri (Spanish explorer)
303. Eastern Colorado was purchased from France by which treaty signed on April 30th, 1803?
Louisiana Purchase
304. By which treaty was most of Colorado (north of the Gila River) granted to the United States in 1848?
Treaty of Guadalupe Hidalgo
305. In which year was the oldest existing Colorado town, San Luis, founded?
1851
306. When was the Territory of Colorado established?
February 28th, 1861
307. When did the Pike's Peak Gold Rush (also called the Colorado Gold Rush) start?
July 1858
308. Who were the fifty-niners?
The gold seekers who streamed into the Pike's Peak Gold Rush
309. When was Colorado admitted to the Union?
August 1st, 1876 (38th)
310. What is the area of Colorado?

104,094 sq mi / 269,837 km^2 (8th)

311. What is the population of Colorado?

5,355,866 (by 2014)

312. What is the topography of Colorado?

Rocky Mountains from north to south, including Sangre de Cristo Mountains and San Juan Mountains; Colorado Eastern Plains in the east; the highest mean altitude in the United States (6,800 ft / 2,073 m)

313. What is the highest point of Colorado, the highest point of the Rocky Mountains?

Mount Elbert (14,433 ft / 4,399 m)

314. What is the lowest point of Colorado?

Arikaree River (3,317 ft / 1,011 m)

315. What are the major rivers in Colorado?

Arkansas River, Colorado River, Rio Grande, and South Platte River

316. What are the major lakes in Colorado?

Grand Lake, Blue Mesa Reservoir, and John Martin Reservoir

317. Which national parks are located in Colorado?

Black Canyon National Park (51 sq mi / 133 km^2), Great Sand Dunes National Park and Preserve (132sq mi / 343 km^2), Mesa Verde National Park (81 sq mi / 211 km^2), and Rocky Mountain National Park (415 sq mi / 1,076 km^2)

318. What is the Black Canyon National Park famous for?

The dark canyon walls from the Precambrian era along the Gunnison River

319. What is the Great Sand Dunes National Park and Preserve famous for?

The tallest dunes in North America (750 ft / 230 m), and neighbor grasslands, shrublands, and wetlands

320. What is the Mesa Verde National Park famous for?

More than 4,000 archaeological sites of the Ancestral Pueblo; cliff dwellings built in the 12th and 13th centuries include the Cliff Palace

321. What is the Rocky Mountain National Park famous for?

Almost 400 miles (640 km) of mountain trails; various species of Colorado wildlife

322. Which mesa in Colorado is the largest mesa in the world?

Grand Mesa (500 sq mi / 1,300 km^2)

323. Colorado contains what percent of the land area of the United States with an altitude over 10,000 ft (3 km)?

75%

324. Which city in Colorado is called the Mile High City?

Denver

325. Which bridge in Colorado was the highest suspension bridge in the world until 2001?

Royal Gorge Bridge (length: 1,260 ft / 384 m, 955 ft / 291 m above the Arkansas River)

326. Which mining village in Colorado is the highest human settlement in the United States?

Climax (11,360 ft / 3,465 m)

327. Who owns more than 1/3 of the land in Colorado?

United States federal government

328. Which street in Denver is the longest continuous street in the United States?

Colfax Avenue

329. Which tunnel in Colorado is the highest auto tunnel in the United States?

Dwight Eisenhower Memorial Tunnel (11,158 ft / 3,401 m)

330. Which city in Colorado is the highest incorporated city in the United States?
Leadville (10,430 ft / 3,200 m)

331. Which city in Colorado is known as the Melon Capital of the World?
Rocky Ford

332. The United States Air Force Academy is located in which city of Colorado?
Colorado Springs

333. What is the climate in Colorado?
Eastern Plains: semi-arid; west of the plains and foothills: most valleys have a semi-arid climate, which becomes an alpine climate at higher elevations; humid microclimates in some areas; extreme weather is common

334. What are the natural resources in Colorado?
Climate, soil, water, oil, coal, molybdenum, sand and gravel, and uranium

335. What are the natural hazards in Colorado?
Thunderstorms, tornadoes, blizzards, heavy snows, and avalanches

336. What are the major industries in Colorado?
Agriculture (wheat, cattle, sheep), tourism (especially skiers), mining (gold, silver), oil, finance, and manufacturing

Connecticut

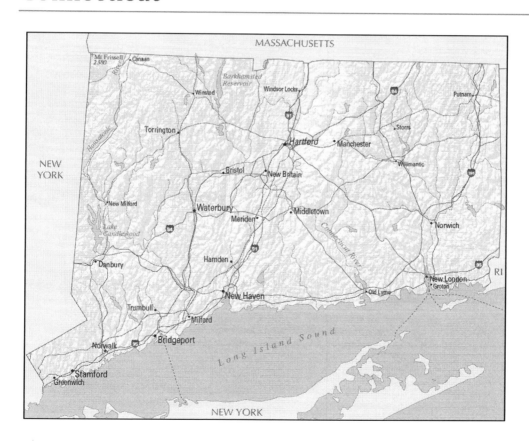

337. Which state borders Connecticut in the north?
Massachusetts

338. Which state borders Connecticut in the east?
Rhode Island

339. Which water body lies to the south of Connecticut?
Long Island Sound

340. Which state borders Connecticut in the west and lies to the south of Connecticut, across Long Island Sound?
New York

341. What are the nicknames of Connecticut?
Constitution State; Nutmeg State; Provisions State; Land of Steady Habits

342. What is the state motto of Connecticut?
He Who Transplanted Still Sustains

343. What is the state song of Connecticut?
Yankee Doodle

344. What is the state tree of Connecticut?
White Oak

345. What is the state flower of Connecticut?
Mountain Laurel

346. What is the state bird of Connecticut?
American Robin

347. What is the state animal of Connecticut?
Sperm Whale

348. What is the state fossil of Connecticut?
Eubrontes Giganteus

349. What is the state insect of Connecticut?
European Mantis

350. What is the state shellfish of Connecticut?
Eastern Oyster

351. What is the state mineral of Connecticut?
Garnet

352. What is the state ship of Connecticut?
USS Nautilus

353. The USS Nautilus, the world's first nuclear powered submarine, was built in which town of Connecticut in 1954?
Groton

354. What is the state folk dance of Connecticut?
     Square Dance
355. What is the state hero of Connecticut?
     Nathan Hale
356. What is the state heroine of Connecticut?
     Prudence Crandall
357. What is the capital of Connecticut?
     Hartford
358. What is the largest city by population in Connecticut?
     Bridgeport
359. What is the largest town by area in Connecticut?
     New Milford
360. Who explored Connecticut in 1614?
     Adriaen Block (Dutch private trader and navigator)
361. What is the oldest town in Connecticut, found as a trading post on September 26th, 1633?
     Windsor (called Dorchester before 1637)
362. What is the Pequot War during 1634 – 1638?
     An armed conflict between the Pequot tribe in Connecticut against an alliance of British colonies with American Indian allies
363. When was the Colony of Connecticut established?
     March 3rd, 1636
364. When was Connecticut admitted to the Union?
     January 9, 1788 (5th)
365. What is the area of Connecticut?
     5,543 sq mi / 14,357 km^2 (48th)
366. What is the population of Connecticut?
     3,596,677 (by 2014)
367. What is the topography of Connecticut?
     Predominantly hilly; Connecticut Valley Lowlands in the center from north to south
368. What is the highest point of Connecticut, located on the border of southwest Massachusetts and northwest Connecticut?
     South slope of Mount Frissell (2,380 ft / 726 m)
369. What is the lowest point of Connecticut?
     Long Island Sound (0 ft / 0 m)
370. How long is the coastline of Connecticut?
     96 mi / 154 km (17th)
371. What are the major rivers in Connecticut?
     Connecticut River, Housatonic River, and Thames River
372. What is the major lake in Connecticut?
     Lake Candlewood
373. Which city in Connecticut is the Insurance Capital of the United States?
     Hartford
374. Which newspaper in Connecticut is the oldest U.S. newspaper still being published?
     Hartford Courant (October 29th, 1764)
375. The first telephone exchange was established in which city in Connecticut, after the

telephone was invented on 1876?

Bridgeport (1877)

376. The first telephone book was published in which city in Connecticut?

New Haven (February 1878)

377. Which town in Connecticut is the first factory town in the United States?

Seymour (1806)

378. Which city in Connecticut is the birthplace of the first Hamburg in the world?

New Haven (Louie's Lunch, 1895)

379. What is the climate in Connecticut?

Cold, stormy winters and relatively mild summers

380. What is the natural resource in Connecticut?

Forest

381. What are the natural hazards in Connecticut?

Blizzards, floods, hurricanes, and tornados

382. What are the major industries in Connecticut?

Agriculture, industry (especially insurance), and tourism

Delaware

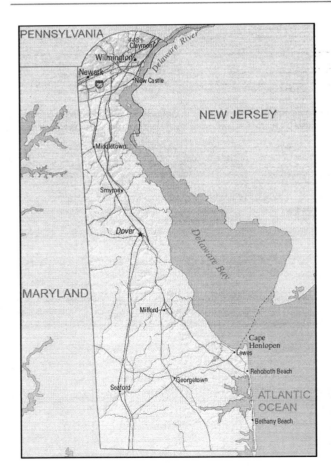

383. Which state borders Delaware in the north?
    Pennsylvania
384. Which state borders Delaware in the west and south?
    Maryland
385. Which river makes up part of the eastern boundary of Delaware?
    Delaware River
386. Which water bodies lie to the east of Delaware?
    Delaware Bay and Atlantic Ocean
387. Which state lies to the east of Delaware, across the Delaware River and Delaware Bay?
    New Jersey
388. What are the nicknames of Delaware?
    First State; Small Wonder; Blue Hen State; Diamond State
389. What is the state motto of Delaware?
    Liberty and Independence
390. What is the state song of Delaware?
    Our Delaware
391. What is the state tree of Delaware?
    American Holly
392. What is the state flower of Delaware?
    Peach Blossom
393. What is the state bird of Delaware?
    Blue Hen Chicken
394. What is the state bug of Delaware?
    Ladybug
395. What is the state fish of Delaware?
    Weakfish
396. What is the state fossil of Delaware?
    Belemnitella Americana
397. What is the state mineral of Delaware?
    Sillimanite
398. What is the state soil of Delaware?
    Greenwich
399. What is the state beverage of Delaware?
    Milk
400. What are the state colors of Delaware?
    Colonial Blue and Buff
401. What is the capital of Delaware?
    Dover (the largest city by area)
402. What is the largest city by population in Delaware?
    Wilmington
403. Who explored Delaware in 1497?
    John Cabot (Italian navigator and explorer)
404. Who explored Delaware in 1609?

Henry Hudson (English navigator and explorer)

405. What was the first European (Dutch) settlement in Delaware, founded on June 3rd, 1631?
Zwaanendael (the present-day Lewes)

406. What was the first Swedish settlement in North America and the principal settlement of the New Sweden colony, founded in 1638?
Fort Christina (later renamed Fort Altena)

407. What is the nickname of Lewes?
First Town in the First State

408. When did Delaware become a British colony?
1704

409. When was Delaware admitted to the Union?
December 7th, 1787, 1819 (1st)

410. What is the area of Delaware?
2,490 sq mi / 6,452 km^2 (49th)

411. What is the population of Delaware?
935,614 (by 2014)

412. What is the topography of Delaware?
Atlantic Coastal Plain; the lowest mean altitude in the United States (60 ft / 18 m)

413. What is the highest point of Delaware?
Ebright Azimuth (448 ft / 137 m)

414. What is the lowest point of Delaware?
Atlantic Ocean (0 ft / 0 m)

415. How long is the coastline of Delaware?
28 mi / 45 km (22th)

416. What are the major rivers in Delaware?
Delaware River, Mispillion River, and Nanticoke River

417. The United States' first scheduled steam railroad began in which city in 1831?
New Castle

418. Which town in Delaware has the motto "The Little Town Too Big for One State"?
Delmar

419. Which city in Delaware is known as the Chemical Capital of the World?
Wilmington

420. What is the climate in Delaware?
Temperate but humid

421. What are the natural resources in Delaware?
Soil, clay, sand and gravel, and Brandywine blue granite

422. What are the natural hazards in Delaware?
Hurricanes and blizzards

423. What are the major industries in Delaware?
Business, agriculture, and tourism

District of Columbia

424. Which state borders the District of Columbia in the southeast, northeast, and northwest?
Maryland

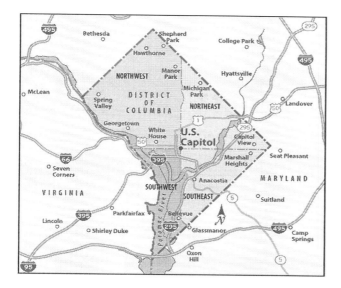
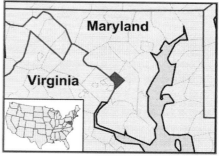

425. Which state borders the District of Columbia in the southwest?
Virginia

426. Which river makes up the southwest boundary of District of Columbia?
Potomac River

427. What are the nicknames of the District of Columbia?
Nation's Capital; America's First City; D.C.

428. What is the official motto of District of Columbia?
Justice for All

429. What is the official song of the District of Columbia?
Star-Spangled Banner

430. What is the official tree of the District of Columbia?
Scarlet Oak

431. What is the official flower of the District of Columbia?
American Beauty Rose

432. What is the official bird of the District of Columbia?
Wood Thrush

433. What is the District of Columbia?
Capital of United States

434. When did Congress pass the Residence Act, which approved the creation of a new national capital?
July 16th, 1790

435. When was the federal city named in honor of George Washington and the district itself named Columbia?
September 9th, 1791

436. When did Congress hold its first session in the District of Columbia?
November 17th, 1800

437. When was the only time since the Revolutionary War that a foreign power (British) captured and occupied the United States capital?
August 24th, 1814

31

438. The land of the District of Columbia was donated by Maryland and Virginia, but the land of which state was returned by Congress in 1846?
Virginia
439. What is the area of the District of Columbia?
68 sq mi (177 km^2)
440. What is the population of the District of Columbia?
658,893 (by 2014)
441. What are the attractions and landmarks of the District of Columbia?
Historic District Capitol Hill: Supreme Court, Union Station, Library of Congress, and United States Capital; Federal Triangle: White House, FBI Building, Ford's Theater, Lincoln Museum, and National Archives
442. What is the highest point of the District of Columbia?
Fort Reno Park in Tenleytown (410 ft / 125 m)
443. What is the lowest point of the District of Columbia?
Potomac River (0 ft / 0 m)
444. What are islands in the District of Columbia?
Theodore Roosevelt Island, Columbia Island, Three Sisters, and Hains Point
445. What are the major rivers in the District of Columbia?
Potomac River and Anacostia River
446. What is the climate in the District of Columbia?
Humid subtropical
447. What are the natural hazards in the District of Columbia?
Hurricanes and tropical storms
448. What are the major industries in the District of Columbia?
Federal Government

Florida

449. Which state borders Florida in the north and west?
Alabama
450. Which state borders Florida in the north?
Georgia
451. Which water body lies to the west and south of Florida?
Gulf of Mexico
452. Which water body lies to the east of Florida?
Atlantic Ocean
453. Which two countries in Caribbean are close to Florida?
The Bahamas and Cuba
454. What is the nickname of Florida?
Sunshine State
455. What is the state motto of Florida?
In God We Trust
456. What is the state song of Florida?
Swanee River

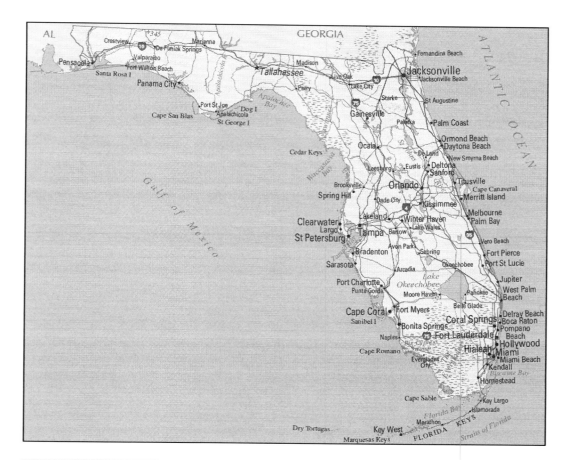

457. What is the state tree of Florida?
Cabbage Palmetto

458. What is the state flower of Florida?
Orange Blossom

459. What is the state wildflower of Florida?
Coreopsis

460. What is the state bird of Florida?
Mockingbird

461. What is the state mammal of Florida?
Florida Panther

462. What is the state marine mammal of Florida?

33

Manatee

463. What is the state salt water mammal of Florida?
Porpoise (Dolphin)

464. What is the state insect of Florida?
Zebra Longwing Butterfly

465. What is the state reptile of Florida?
Alligator

466. What is the state saltwater fish of Florida?
Sailfish

467. What is the state freshwater fish of Florida?
Largemouth Bass

468. What is the state shell of Florida?
Horse Conch

469. What is the state beverage of Florida?
Orange Juice

470. What is the state stone of Florida?
Agatized Coral

471. What is the state gem of Florida?
Moonstone

472. What is the capital of Florida?
Tallahassee

473. What is the largest city by population and area in Florida?
Jacksonville

474. Who landed in Florida on April 3rd, 1513?
Juan Ponce de León (Spanish conquistador)

475. What present-day areas were included in the Spanish Florida, established in 1513?
Florida, southern Georgia, southern Alabama, southeastern Louisiana, and other areas along the northern coast of the Gulf of Mexico

476. Which city in Florida is the oldest continuously inhabited city in the United States, founded by Pedro Menéndez de Avilés (Spanish explorer and admiral)?
St. Augustine (1565)

477. In 1763, Spain traded Florida to Britain in exchange for control of which city?
Havana (in Cuba)

478. In which year, Spain regained control of Florida?
1783

479. Which part of Florida was claimed by the United States according to the Louisiana Purchase in 1803?
West Florida and Pensacola

480. Spain ceded Florida to the United States as part of which treaty signed on February 22th, 1819?
Adams-Onís Treaty

481. When was the Territory of Florida established?
March 30th, 1822

482. When was Florida admitted to the Union?
March 3, 1845 (27th)

483. During which period did Florida secede from the Union?
    1861 – 1865
484. What is the area of Florida?
    65,755 sq mi / 170,304 km^2 (22nd)
485. What is the population of Florida?
    19,893,297 (by 2014)
486. What is the topography of Florida?
    Low-lying and fairly level
487. What is the highest point of Florida, located in the Florida Ridge Hills?
    Britton Hill (345 ft / 105 m, the lowest state highpoint in the United States)
488. What is the lowest point of Florida?
    Gulf of Mexico (0 ft / 0 m)
489. How long is the coastline of Florida?
    1,350 mi / 2,173 km (2nd)
490. What are the major rivers in Florida?
    St. Johns River, St. Marys River, and Suwannee River
491. What are the major lakes in Florida?
    Lake Okeechobee and Lake George
492. Which national parks are located in Florida?
    Biscayne National Park (207 sq mi / 700 km²), Dry Tortugas National Park (101 sq mi / 262 km^2), and Everglades National Park (2,357 sq mi / 6,105 km²)
493. What is the Biscayne National Park famous for?
    Mangrove forest, the Bay, the Keys, and coral reefs
494. What is the Dry Tortugas National Park famous for?
    Coral reefs and shipwrecks
495. What is the Everglades National Park famous for?
    The largest subtropical wilderness in the United States
496. Which city in Florida is known as the Venice of America?
    Fort Lauderdale (185 mi / 298 km long waterways)
497. Which city in Florida is known as the Heart of Florida?
    Haines City
498. Which city in Florida is known as the Shark Tooth Capital of the World?
    Venice
499. Which city in Florida is known as the Space City?
    Titusville
500. Walt Disney World, the world's busiest theme park, in located in which city of Florida?
    Orlando
501. Which village in Florida is known as the Sports Fishing Capital of the World?
    Islamorada
502. Which island in Florida is known as the Dive Capital of the World?
    Key Largo
503. Which island in Florida has the highest average temperature in the United States?
    Key West
504. Which city in Florida is the hottest city in the United States, measured by the average annual temperature?

Key West (78 °F / 25 °C)

505. What are the nicknames of Key West?
Conch Republic; Southernmost City in the Continental United States

506. Which space center is located on Cape Canaveral?
Kennedy Space Center

507. Which bridge in Florida became the longest cable-stayed span in the United States, the longest concrete span of its type in the Western Hemisphere, and the 3rd longest cable-stayed bridge in the world, when first completed in 1989?
Dame Point Bridge

508. Which river sailboat race is the longest in the world, which runs 42 mi (68 km) from Palatka to Jacksonville along the St. Johns River?
Annual Mug Race

509. Florida is the only state that has two rivers with the same name. One is in north central Florida and the other one in central Florida. What are their names?
Withlacoochee

510. What is the climate in Florida?
North of Lake Okeechobee is humid subtropical; south of Lake Okeechobee is tropical

511. What are the natural resources in Florida?
Sandy beaches, sunny climate, thick forests, phosphate, limestone, ilmenite, rutile, and zircon

512. What are the natural hazards in Florida?
Hurricanes, tropical storms, tropical depressions, tornadoes, wildfires, and floods

513. What are the major industries in Florida?
Tourism, agriculture, and electronics

Georgia

514. Which states border Georgia in the north?
Tennessee and North Carolina

515. Which state borders Georgia in the east?
South Carolina

516. Which state borders Georgia in the south?
Florida

517. Which state borders Georgia in the west?
Alabama

518. Which river makes up part of the western boundary of Georgia?
Chattahoochee River

519. Which water body lies to the east of Georgia?
Atlantic Ocean

520. What are the nicknames of Georgia?
Peach State; Cracker State; Empire State of the South

521. What is the state motto of Georgia?
Wisdom, Justice, Moderation

522. What is the state song of Georgia?
Georgia on My Mind

523. What is the state tree of Georgia?
     Live Oak
524. What is the state flower of Georgia?
     Cherokee Rose
525. What is the state wildflower of Georgia?
     Azalea
526. What is the state bird of Georgia?
     Brown Thrasher
527. What is the state game bird of Georgia?
     Bobwhite
528. What is the state marine mammal of Georgia?
     Right Whale
529. What is the state possum of Georgia?
     Pogo Possum
530. What is the state insect of Georgia?
     Honeybee
531. What is the state reptile of Georgia?
     Gopher Tortoise
532. What is the state fish of Georgia?
     Largemouth Bass
533. What is the state shell of Georgia?

Knobbed Whelk

534. What is the state fossil of Georgia?
Shark Tooth

535. What is the state mineral of Georgia?
Staurolite

536. What is the state gem of Georgia?
Quartz

537. What is the capital of Georgia?
Atlanta (the largest city by population)

538. What is the largest city by area in Georgia?
Augusta (307 sq mi / 793 km^2)

539. Who explored Georgia in 1540?
Hernando de Soto (Spanish explorer)

540. Who established numerous forts and missions in Georgia in 1565?
Pedro Menendez (Spanish explorer)

541. Who founded Georgia Colony on April 21st, 1733?
James Oglethorpe (British general, Member of Parliament, and philanthropist)

542. When was Georgia admitted to the Union?
January 2nd, 1788 (4th)

543. Which city in Georgia is the 2nd oldest continuously inhabited city in the United States?
St. Mary's (1792)

544. During which period did Georgia secede from the Union?
1861 – 1865

545. What is the area of Georgia?
52,419 sq mi / 135,765 km^2 (30th)

546. What is the population of Georgia?
10,097,343 (by 2014)

547. What is the topography of Georgia?
Appalachians Mountains in the northwest; Blue Ridge Mountains in the northeast; Piedmont Plateau in the central; Coastal Plain in the south; Golden Isles of Georgia along the coast

548. What is the highest point of Georgia, located in the Blue Ridge Mountains?
Brasstown Bald (4,784 ft / 1,458 m)

549. What is the lowest point of Georgia?
Atlantic Ocean (0 ft / 0 m)

550. Which four barrier islands are parts of the Golden Isles of Georgia?
St. Simons Island, Sea Island, Jekyll Island, and Little St. Simons Island

551. Which swamp, located in Georgia and Florida, is the largest peat-based "blackwater" swamp in North America?
Okefenokee Swamp (684 sq mi / 1,770 km²)

552. Georgia is the nation's number one producer of which three Ps food?
Peanuts, pecans, and peaches

553. Which university in Georgia was the first chartered public university in the United States by chartering in 1785?
University in Georgia

554. Which town in Georgia was the site of the first Gold Rush (1828) in the United States?
Auraria

555. Coca-Cola was first sold in Jacob's Pharmacy of which city in Georgia?
Atlanta

556. Berry College of which city in Georgia has the world's largest college campus?
Rome

557. Marshall Forest of which city in Georgia is the only natural forest within a city limits in the United States?
Rome

558. Which city in Georgia is known as the City of Roses?
Thomasville

559. Wesleyan College of which city in Georgia was the first college in the world chartered to grant degrees to women?
Macon

560. How long is the coastline of Georgia?
161 mi / 85 km (16th)

561. What are the major rivers in Georgia?
Chattahoochee River, Savannah River, and Suwannee River

562. What are the major lakes in Georgia?
Lake Sidney Lanier, Clark Hill Lake, West Point Lake, and Lake Hartwell

563. Which city in Georgia is known as the Chicken Capital of the World?
Gainesville

564. What is the climate in Georgia?
Humid subtropical

565. What are the natural resources in Georgia?
Clays, large granite deposits, marble, feldspar, some gold, barite, manganese, bauxite, fuller's earth, kaolin, bentonites, coal, kyanite, limestone, mica, forests, and water

566. What are the natural hazards in Georgia?
Hurricanes and tornados

567. What are the major industries in Georgia?
Textiles, timber, and agriculture

Hawaii

568. Which body of water is Hawaii located?
Pacific Ocean

569. What is the nickname of Hawaii?
Aloha State

570. What is the state motto of Hawaii?
The Life of the Land is Perpetuated in Righteousness

571. What is the state song of Hawaii?
Hawaii's Own True Sons

572. What is the state tree of Hawaii?
Kukui

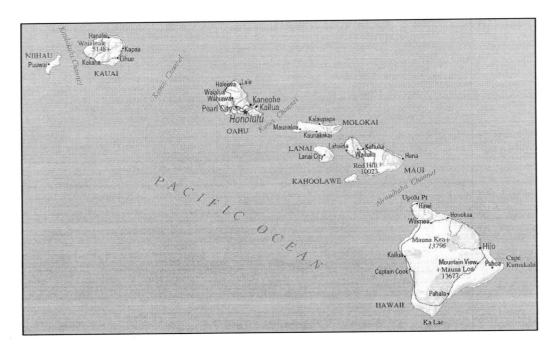

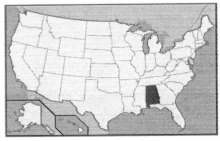

573. What is the state flower of Hawaii?
Hibiscus
574. What is the state bird of Hawaii?
Nene (Hawaiian Goose)
575. What is the state mammal of Hawaii?
Monk Seal
576. What is the state marine mammal of Hawaii?
Humpback Whale
577. What is the state fish of Hawaii?
Humuhumunukunuku Apua'a (Reef Triggerfish)
578. What is the state gem of Hawaii?
Black Coral
579. What is the state soil of Hawaii?
Hilo
580. What is the capital of Hawaii?
Honolulu (the largest city by population and area)
581. Why does Honolulu claim to be the largest city in the world?

Because the state of Hawaii stated that the entire island belongs to Honolulu that makes the entire Oahu island Honolulu, plus bits of other islands

582. Which county in Hawaii is the smallest county by area in the United States?
Kalawao County (13 sq mi / 34 km^2)

583. What is the oldest unincorporated city in the Hawaiian archipelago?
Hilo

584. Who first visited Hawaii and named it the Sandwich Islands in 1778?
James Cook (English explorer)

585. In which year was the Kingdom of Hawaii established?
1795

586. In which year was the Republic of Hawaii established?
1894

587. In which year was the Territory of Hawaii established?
1898

588. When was Hawaii admitted to the Union?
August 21st, 1959 (50th)

589. When did Japan attack Pearl Harbor, and brought the United States into World War II?
December 7th, 1941

590. What is the area of Hawaii?
10,931 sq mi / 28,311 km^2 (43rd)

591. What is the population of Hawaii?
1,419,561 (by 2014)

592. What is the topography of Hawaii?
Archipelago of 19 islands and atolls, numerous smaller islets, and undersea seamounts; islands are rugged and volcanic

593. What is the highest point on Hawaii Island, the biggest island in the Hawaiian Islands?
Mauna Kea (13,796 ft / 4,205 m, world's tallest mountain if measured from the sea floor - 33,500 ft / 10,200 m)

594. What is the highest point on Maui Island, the 2nd biggest island in the Hawaiian Islands?
Haleakala (10,023 ft / 3,055 m)

595. What is the highest point on Oahu Island, the 3rd biggest island in the Hawaiian Islands?
Mount Kaala (4,025 ft / 1,227 m)

596. What is the highest point on Kauai Island, the 4th biggest island in the Hawaiian Islands?
Kawaikini (5,243 ft / 1,598 m)

597. What is the lowest point of Hawaii?
Pacific Ocean (0 ft / 0 m)

598. How long is the coastline of Hawaii?
750 mi / 1,207 km (4th)

599. What are the major rivers in Hawaii?
Wailuku River and Anahulu River

600. What is the major lake in Hawaii?
Salt Lake

601. Which national parks are located in Hawaii?
Haleaka National Park (45 sq mi / 118 km^2) and Hawaii Volcanoes National Park (505 sq mi / 1,309 km^2)

602. What is the Haleaka National Park, located on Hawaii Island, famous for?
Mauna Loa (the largest volcano on Earth in terms of volume and area covered) and Kilauea (one of the most active volcanoes on Earth)
603. What is the Hawaii Volcanoes National Park, located on Maui Island, famous for?
The Haleakala Crater, the world's largest dormant volcano, containing many cinder cones, Hosmer's Grove of alien trees, and the native Hawaiian Goose; the Kipahulu village with numerous pools containing freshwater fish
604. Which cliffs on Moloka Island are the highest sea cliffs in the world?
Kalaupapa Cliffs (3,315 ft / 1,010 m)
605. Which waterfall on Hawaii Island is the highest waterfall in Hawaii?
Hiilawe Falls (1,600 ft / 488 m)
606. Which palace in Hawaii is the only royal palace in the United States?
Iolani Palace
607. In which year was coffee first planted in Kona?
1829
608. In which year was first sugar plantation established in Koloa?
1835
609. In which year were macadamia nuts introduced to Hawaii?
1881
610. In which year were pineapples first planted in Kona?
1885
611. In which year did James Drummond Dole plant first pineapples and establish Hawaiian Pineapple Company?
1901
612. Which part of Hawaii observes the daylight savings time change?
None
613. Which city in Hawaii is the wettest city in the United States, measured by the average annual precipitation in inches and number of days per year with rain?
Hilo
614. What is the climate in Hawaii?
Tropical
615. What are the natural resources in Hawaii?
Beaches, mild, warm climate, deep topsoil, underground water, and soil rich in titanium oxide
616. What are the natural hazards in Hawaii?
Earthquakes, floods, tsunamis, hurricanes, tidal waves, and volcanic eruptions
617. What are the major industries in Hawaii?
Tourism and agriculture (bananas, pineapples, macadamia nuts, and taro)

Idaho

618. Which state borders Idaho in the northeast?
Montana
619. Which state borders Idaho in the east?
Wyoming

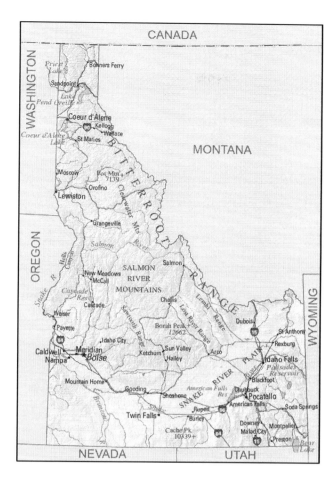

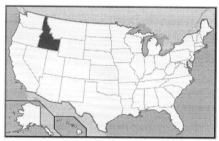

620. Which states border Idaho in the west?
Washington and Oregon

621. Which states border Idaho in the south?
Nevada and Utah

622. Which country borders Idaho in the north?
Canada

623. Which river makes up part of the west boundary of Idaho?
Snake River

624. What are the nicknames of Idaho?
Gem State; Spud Government

625. What is the state motto of Idaho?
May it Endure Forever

626. What is the state song of Idaho?
Here We Have Idaho

627. What is the state tree of Idaho?
Western White Pine

628. What is the state flower of Idaho?
Syringa

629. What is the state bird of Idaho?
Mountain Bluebird
630. What is the state horse of Idaho?
Appaloosa
631. What is the state fish of Idaho?
Cutthroat Trout
632. What is the state insect of Idaho?
Monarch Butterfly
633. What is the state fossil of Idaho?
Hagerman Horse Fossil
634. What is the state gemstone of Idaho?
Idaho Star Garnet
635. What is the state dance of Idaho?
Square Dance
636. What is the capital of Idaho?
Boise (the largest city by population and area)
637. Which group built the first organized town in Idaho, Franklin, in 1860?
Mormons
638. When was the Territory of Idaho established, split from the Territory of Washington?
March 4th, 1863
639. When was Idaho admitted to the Union?
July 3rd, 1890 (43rd)
640. What is the area of Idaho?
83,570 sq mi / 216,632 km² (14th)
641. What is the population of Idaho?
1,634,464 (by 2014)
642. What is the topography of Idaho?
Rocky Mountains cross most part; Salmon River Mountains in the center; Bitterroot Range on the border with Montana; Snake River Plain in the south
643. What is the highest point of Idaho, located in the Lost River Range?
Borah Peak (12,668 ft / 3,861 m)
644. Which city calls itself the Top of Idaho because it is the nearest city to Borah Peak?
Mackay
645. What is the lowest point of Idaho?
Snake River (710 ft / 217 m)
646. What are the major rivers in Idaho?
Snake River, Clark Fork/Pend Oreille River, Clearwater River, and Salmon River.
647. What are the major lakes in Idaho?
Lake Pend Oreille, American Falls Reservoir, and Coeur d'Alene Lake
648. Which national park is located in Idaho?
Yellowstone National Park (in Wyoming, Montana, and Idaho, 3,472 sq mi / 8,987 km²)
649. Which state park contains the tallest single structured sand dune (470 ft /143 m) in the North America?
Bruneau Dunes State Park
650. Which area in Idaho is home to the world's most dense population of nesting eagles, hawks,

and falcons?
Snake River Birds of Prey National Conservation Area

651. Which canyon on the Bruneau River is 1,300 ft (396 m) wide, 800 ft (244 m) deep and 60 mi (97 km) long?
Bruneau Canyon

652. Which canyon in Idaho is the deepest canyon in the United States?
Hell's Canyon (7,993 ft / 2,436 m)

653. Which city in the Gem Valley is most famous for its certified seed potatoes?
Grace

654. Which city in Idaho is famous for hot springs?
Lava Hot Springs

655. Which city in Idaho boasts the largest man-made geyser in the world?
Soda Springs

656. Which city in Idaho is located at the confluence of the Snake River and the Clearwater River?
Lewiston

657. Which waterfall in Idaho is called the Niagara of the West?
Shoshone Falls

658. What is the climate in Idaho?
Cold, snowy winters; brief, mild summers

659. What are the natural resources in Idaho?
Fertile topsoil and abundant water

660. What are the natural hazards in Idaho?
Wildfires and earthquakes

661. What are the major industries in Idaho?
Agriculture (potatoes, wheat, sugar beets, barley), lumber, and mining

Illinois

662. Which state borders Illinois in the north?
Wisconsin

663. Which states border Illinois in the west?
Iowa and Missouri

664. Which state borders Illinois in the south?
Kentucky

665. Which state borders Illinois in the east?
Indiana

666. Which river makes up the western boundary of Illinois?
Mississippi River

667. Which river makes up the southeastern boundary of Illinois?
Ohio River

668. Which river makes up part of the eastern boundary of Illinois?
Wabash River

669. Which water body lies to the northeast of Illinois?
Lake Michigan

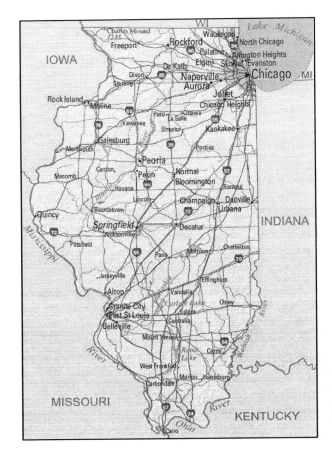

670. Which state lies to the east of Illinois, across the Lake Michigan?
   Michigan

671. What are the nicknames of Illinois?
   Land of Lincoln; Prairie State

672. What is the state motto of Illinois?
   State Sovereignty, National Union

673. What is the state song of Illinois?
   Illinois

674. What is the state tree of Illinois?
   White Oak

675. What is the state flower of Illinois?
   Illinois Native (Purple) Violet

676. What is the state bird of Illinois?
   Cardinal

677. What is the state mammal of Illinois?
   White-tailed Deer

678. What is the state insect of Illinois?
   Monarch Butterfly

679. What is the state fish of Illinois?

Bluegill

680. What is the state fossil of Illinois?
Tully Monster

681. What is the state mineral of Illinois?
Fluorite

682. What is the capital of Illinois?
Springfield

683. What is the largest city by population and area in Illinois?
Chicago

684. Who explored Illinois in 1673?
Jacques Marquette (French explorer) and Louis Jolliet (French missionary)

685. Which city became the first European (French) settlement in Illinois, founded in 1680?
Peoria

686. In which year did Illinois become a French colony?
1717

687. In which year did the Britain control Illinois after the decisive victory of the French and Indian War?
1763

688. In which year did the United States control Illinois after the American Revolutionary War?
1783

689. When was the Territory Northwest of the River Ohio, including Illinois, established?
July 13th, 1787

690. When was the Territory of Indiana, including Illinois, established?
July 4th, 1800

691. When was the Territory of Illinois split from the Territory of Indiana?
March 1st, 1809

692. When was Illinois admitted to the Union?
December 3rd, 1818 (21st)

693. In which year was Illinois the first state to ratify the 13th Amendment to the Constitution abolishing slavery?
1865

694. What is the area of Illinois?
57,914 sq mi /149,998 km^2 (25th)

695. What is the population of Illinois?
12,880,580 (by 2014)

696. What is the topography of Illinois?
Entirely in the Interior Plains

697. What is the highest point of Illinois?
Charles Mound (1,235 ft / 377 m)

698. What is the lowest point of Illinois?
Mississippi River (279 ft / 85 m)

699. What are the major rivers in Illinois?
Mississippi River, Ohio River, Illinois River, and Wabash River

700. Which color is the Chicago River dyed on Saint Patrick's Day?
Green

701. What are the major lakes in Illinois?
Lake Michigan and Rend Lake
702. Which city in Illinois is the home to the Superman, a movie creation?
Metropolis
703. Which city in Illinois is home to the first McDonald's?
Des Plaines
704. Which building in Chicago was the first steel frame skyscraper, built in 1885?
Home Insurance Building
705. Which building in Chicago is the tallest building in North America, built in 1974?
Willis Tower (formally called Sears Tower, 1,451 ft / 442 m)
706. What is the climate in Illinois?
Humid continental
707. What are the natural resources in Illinois?
Fertile soil, coal, and oil
708. What are the natural hazards in Illinois?
Earthquakes, hurricanes, tornados, blizzards, floods, heat and cold waves
709. What are the major industries in Illinois?
Agriculture (corn, soybeans, wheat, oats, barley, rye, sorghum), cattle, manufacturing, and mining

Indiana

710. Which state borders Indiana in the north?
Michigan
711. Which state borders Indiana in the east?
Ohio
712. Which state borders Indiana in the south?
Kentucky
713. Which state borders Indiana in the west?
Illinois
714. Which river makes up the southern boundary of Indiana?
Ohio River
715. Which river makes up part of the western boundary of Indiana?
Wabash River
716. Which water body lies to the northwest of Indiana?
Lake Michigan
717. What is the nickname of Indiana?
Hoosier State
718. What is the state motto of Indiana?
The Crossroads of America
719. What is the state song of Indiana?
On the Banks of the Wabash, Far Away
720. What is the state tree of Indiana?
Tulip Tree

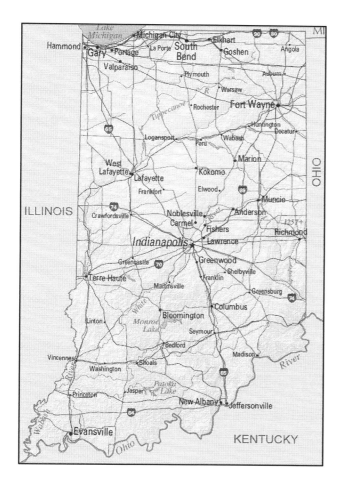

721. What is the state flower of Indiana?
Peony

722. What is the state bird of Indiana?
Cardinal

723. What is the state stone of Indiana?
Salem Limestone

724. What is the capital of Indiana?
Indianapolis (the largest city by population and area)

725. Who explored Indiana in 1679?
Robert de LaSalle (French explorer)

726. What was the oldest continually inhabited European (French) settlement in Indiana, founded in 1732?
Vincennes

727. In which year did the Britain control Indiana after the decisive victory of the French and Indian War?
1763

728. In which year did the United States control Indiana after the American Revolutionary War?
1783

729. When was the Territory Northwest of the River Ohio, including Indiana, established?
July 13th, 1787

730. When was the Territory of Indiana established?
July 4th, 1800

731. When was Indiana admitted to the Union?
December 11th, 1816 (19th)

732. What is the area of Indiana?
36,418 sq mi / 94,321 km^2 (38th)

733. What is the population of Indiana?
6,596,855 (by 2014)

734. What is the topography of Indiana?
Gently rolling forest and prairie, with a few hilly area in the north and central; many natural lakes in the northeast; many wetland areas and unique sand dune landscapes in the northwest; very hilly and heavily forested in the south

735. What is the highest point of Indiana, located in the eastern central Indiana?
Hoosier Hill (1,257 ft / 383 m)

736. What is the lowest point of Indiana?
Ohio River and mouth of Wabash River (320 ft /98 m)

737. What are the major rivers in Indiana?
Ohio River, Wabash River, White River, and Tippecanoe River

738. What are the major lakes in Indiana?
Mississinewa Lake and Lake Michigan

739. Which city in Indiana was once known as the Circus Capital of America?
Peru

740. The Indianapolis 500, the auto race, is held every Memorial Day weekend in which city of Indiana?
Indianapolis

741. The first professional baseball game was played in which city of Indiana on May 4th, 1871?
Fort Wayne

742. What is the climate in Indiana?
Humid continental

743. What are the natural resources in Indiana?
Fertile soil, mineral deposits, and abundant water

744. What are the natural hazards in Indiana?
Thunderstorms, ice storms, blizzards, tornadoes, flooding, and occasionally earthquakes

745. What are the major industries in Indiana?
Agriculture (corn, soybeans, wheat), manufacturing, mining (coal, limestone), and steel-making

Iowa

746. Which state borders Iowa in the north?
Minnesota

747. Which states border Iowa in the east?
Wisconsin and Illinois

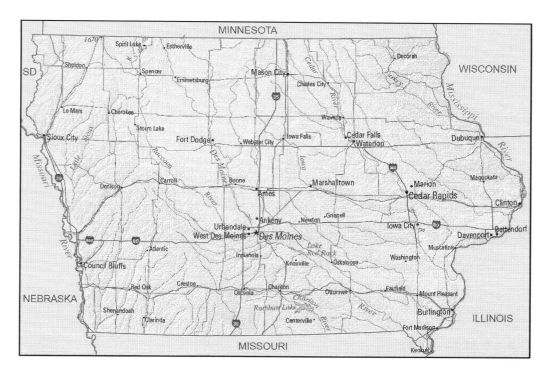

748. Which state borders Iowa in the south?
     Missouri
749. Which states border Iowa in the west?
     South Dakota and Nebraska
750. Which river makes up the eastern boundary of Illinois?
     Mississippi River
751. Which rivers make up the western boundary of Illinois?
     Missouri River and Big Sioux River
752. What is the nickname of Iowa?
     Hawkeye State
753. What is the state motto of Iowa?
     Our Liberties We Prize and Our Rights We Will Maintain
754. What is the state song of Iowa?
     The Song of Iowa
755. What is the state tree of Iowa?

Oak
756. What is the state flower of Iowa?
Wild Rose
757. What is the state bird of Iowa?
Eastern Goldfinch
758. What is the state rock of Iowa?
Geode
759. What is the capital of Iowa?
Des Moines (the largest city by population and area)
760. Who explored Iowa in 1673?
Jacques Marquette (French explorer) and Louis Jolliet (French missionary)
761. Who navigated the Mississippi River and claimed for France all lands drained by the river and its tributaries, including Iowa, in 1682?
Robert de LaSalle (French explorer)
762. France transferred Iowa to which country in 1762?
Spain
763. Which city became the first European (Quebecois) settlement in Iowa, founded in 1788?
Dubuque
764. Spain transferred Iowa to which country in 1800?
France
765. Iowa was purchased from France by which treaty signed on April 30th, 1803?
Louisiana Purchase
766. When was the Territory of Iowa established, split from the Territory of Wisconsin?
July 4th, 1838
767. When was Iowa admitted to the Union?
December 28th, 1846 (29th)
768. What is the area of Iowa?
56,272 sq mi / 145,743 km^2 (26th)
769. What is the population of Iowa?
3,107,126 (by 2014)
770. What is the topography of Iowa?
Mostly rolling hills; only state whose east and west borders are 100% formed by water
771. What is the highest point of Iowa?
Hawkeye Point (1,670 ft / 509 m)
772. What is the lowest point of Iowa?
Mississippi River at Keokuk (480 ft / 146 m)
773. What are the major rivers in Iowa?
Mississippi River, Des Moines River, Missouri River, Cedar River, and Iowa River
774. What is the major lake in Iowa?
Lake Red Rock
775. Which town is Iowa's only town on an island?
Sabula
776. What is the climate in Iowa?
Humid continental
777. What are the natural resources in Iowa?

Fertile topsoil and abundant water

778. What are the natural hazards in Iowa?
Tornados and floods

779. What are the major industries in Iowa?
Agriculture (corn, soybeans, hogs, pigs), food manufacturing, and insurance

Kansas

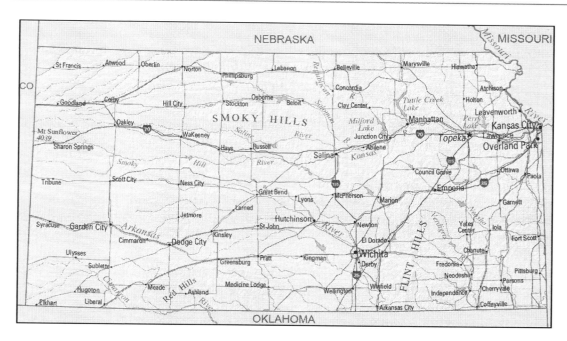

780. Which state borders Kansas in the north?
Nebraska

781. Which state borders Kansas in the northeast and east?
Missouri

782. Which state borders Kansas in the south?
Oklahoma

783. Which state borders Kansas in the west?
Colorado

784. Which river makes up the northeastern boundary of Kansas?

Mississippi River

785. What is the nickname of Kansas?
Sunflower State

786. What is the state motto of Kansas?
To the Stars Through Difficulties

787. What is the state song of Kansas?
Home on the Range

788. What is the state tree of Kansas?
Cottonwood

789. What is the state flower of Kansas?
Sunflower

790. What is the state bird of Kansas?
Western Meadowlark

791. What is the state animal of Kansas?
Buffalo

792. What is the state reptile of Kansas?
Ornate Box Turtle

793. What is the state amphibian of Kansas?
Barred Tiger Salamander

794. What is the state insect of Kansas?
Honeybee

795. What is the state soil of Kansas?
Harney Series

796. What is the capital of Kansas?
Topeka

797. What is the largest city by population and area in Kansas?
Wichita

798. Who explored Kansas in 1541?
Francisco Vásquez de Coronado (Spanish conquistador)

799. Who navigated the Mississippi River and claimed for France all lands drained by the river and its tributaries, including Kansas, in 1682?
Robert de LaSalle (French explorer)

800. Kansas was purchased from France by which treaty signed on April 30th, 1803?
Louisiana Purchase

801. By which treaty was southwestern of Kansas granted to the United States in 1848?
Treaty of Guadalupe Hidalgo

802. Which city, founded in 1854, was the first incorporated city in Kansas?
Leavenworth

803. When was the Territory of Kansas established?
May 30th, 1854

804. When was Kansas admitted to the Union?
January 29th, 1861 (34th)

805. What is the area of Kansas?
82,277 sq mi / 213,096 km^2 (15th)

806. What is the population of Kansas?

2,904,021 (by 2014)

807. What is the topography of Kansas?
Great Plains in the western two-thirds; hills and forests in the eastern third; the land gradually rises from east to west

808. What is the highest point of Kansas, located in the Appalachian Mountains?
Mount Sunflower (4,039 ft / 1,232 m)

809. What is the lowest point of Kansas?
Verdigris River (679 ft / 207 m)

810. What are the major rivers in Kansas?
Kansas River, Republican River, Smoky Hill River, Arkansas River, and Missouri River

811. What are the major lakes in Kansas?
Tuttle Creek Reservoir, Cheney Reservoir, and Waconda Lake

812. Which city in Kansas is the windiest city in the United States?
Dodge City

813. Which city in Kansas is nicknamed the Salt City because it was built above some of the richest salt deposits in the world?
Hutchinson

814. The Pizza Hut restaurants opened its first store in which city of Kansas in 1958?
Wichita

815. Which city in Kansas is the geographical center of the 48 contiguous United States?
Lebanon

816. Which county in Kansas is known as the Wheat Capital of the World?
Sumner

817. Which railroad bridge in Kansas (1905 – 1972), was the longest of its kind in the world?
Rock Island Bridge (1,200 ft / 366 m)

818. What is the climate in Kansas?
Humid continental in the western two-thirds; semiarid steppe in the eastern third; humid subtropical in the far south-central and southeast

819. What are the natural resources in Kansas?
Fertile soil and mineral deposits (Petroleum, natural gas, clays, gypsum, helium, natural gas liquids, salt, sand and gravel, stone)

820. What are the natural hazards in Kansas?
Floods; winter storms, and tornados

821. What are the major industries in Kansas?
Agriculture (wheat and other grains), aircraft manufacturing, and automobile manufacturing

Kentucky

822. Which state borders Kentucky in the southeast?
Virginia

823. Which state borders Kentucky in the east?
West Virginia

824. Which state borders Kentucky in the north and northeast?
Ohio

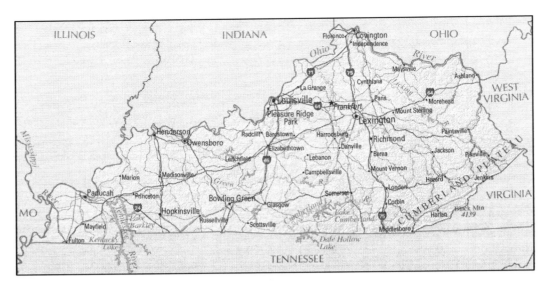

825. Which state borders Kentucky in the south?
   Tennessee
826. Which states border Kentucky in the northwest?
   Illinois and Indiana
827. Which state borders Kentucky in the west?
   Missouri
828. Which river makes up the northwest, northern, and northeast boundaries of Kentucky?
   Ohio River
829. Which river makes up the western boundary of Kentucky?
   Mississippi River
830. What is the nickname of Kentucky?
   Bluegrass State
831. What is the state motto of Kentucky?
   United We Stand, Divided We Fall
832. What is the state slogan of Kentucky?
   Unbridled Spirit
833. What is the state song of Kentucky?
   My Old Kentucky Home
834. What is the state tree of Kentucky?
   Tulip Tree

835. What was the state tree of Kentucky before 1976?
Kentucky Coffee Tree
836. What is the state flower of Kentucky?
Goldenrod
837. What is the state bird of Kentucky?
Cardinal
838. What is the state wild animal of Kentucky?
Gray Squirrel
839. What is the state horse of Kentucky?
Thoroughbred
840. What is the state fish of Kentucky?
Kentucky Bass
841. What is the state insect of Kentucky?
Viceroy Butterfly
842. What is the state fossil of Kentucky?
Brachiopod
843. What is the state gemstone of Kentucky?
Freshwater Pearl
844. What is the capital of Kentucky?
Frankfort
845. What is the largest city by population and area in Kentucky?
Louisville
846. Who arrived to survey the Kentucky area in 1654?
Abram Wood (Colonel of Virginia)
847. Which country claimed Kentucky in 1720s?
France
848. What is the oldest city in Kentucky, founded on June 16th, 1774?
Harrodsburg
849. When was Kentucky admitted to the Union, seceding from Virginia?
June 1st, 1792 (15th)
850. What is the area of Kentucky?
40,409 sq mi / 104,659 km^2 (37th)
851. What is the population of Kentucky?
4,413,457 (by 2014)
852. What is the topography of Kentucky?
Cumberland Plateau in the east; Bluegrass Region in the north-central; Pennyroyal Plateau in the south-central and western
853. What is the highest point of Kentucky, located in the Cumberland Mountains?
Black Mountain (4,145 ft / 1,263 m)
854. What is the lowest point of Kentucky?
Kentucky Bend (257 ft / 78 m)
855. What are the major rivers in Kentucky?
Ohio River, Mississippi River, Cumberland River, Kentucky River, and Green River
856. What are the major lakes in Kentucky?
Lake Cumberland, Kentucky Lake, and Lake Barkley

857. Which national park is located in Kentucky?
Mammoth Cave National Park (83 sq mi / 214 km^2)

858. What is the Mammoth Cave National Park famous for?
The world's longest passageways (392 mi / 631 km)

859. Which city is the site of the Kentucky Derby, the oldest continuously held horse race in the United States?
Louisville (1875)

860. Teacher Mary S. Wilson held the first observance of Mother's Day in which city of Kentucky in 1887, and later was made a national holiday in 1916?
Henderson

861. The song "Happy Birthday to You" was the creation of two Louisville sisters in which year?
1893

862. Which city is the site of the first Kentucky Fried Chicken restaurant owned and operated by Colonel Sanders?
Corbin (1930)

863. Which city in Kentucky is the only city in the United States built within a meteor crater?
Middlesboro

864. Which city in Kentucky is the site of the world's largest free-swinging bell known as the World Peace Bell?
Newport

865. Which city in Kentucky stores the world's largest amount of gold (more than $6 billion)?
Fort Knox

866. The Cathedral Basilica of the Assumption, located in which city of Kentucky, has 82 stained-glass windows including the world's largest hand-blown one (24 ft / 7 m x 67 ft / 20 m, with 134 life-sized figures)?
Covington

867. Which waterfall in Kentucky is the only waterfall in the world that regularly displays a moonbow, a rainbow produced by the light of the moon?
Cumberland Falls

868. Which boat tour in Kentucky claims the shortest and deepest underground river in the world?
Lost River Cave and Valley

869. What is the climate in Kentucky?
Humid subtropical

870. What are the natural resources in Kentucky?
Rich soil and abundant coal deposits

871. What are the natural hazards in Kentucky?
Earthquakes, tornados, floods, and blizzards

872. What are the major industries in Kentucky?
Agriculture (tobacco, corn, peanuts, wheat), mining (anthracite coal), horse-raising, whiskey manufacturing, automobile and truck manufacturing, and chemical manufacturing

Louisiana

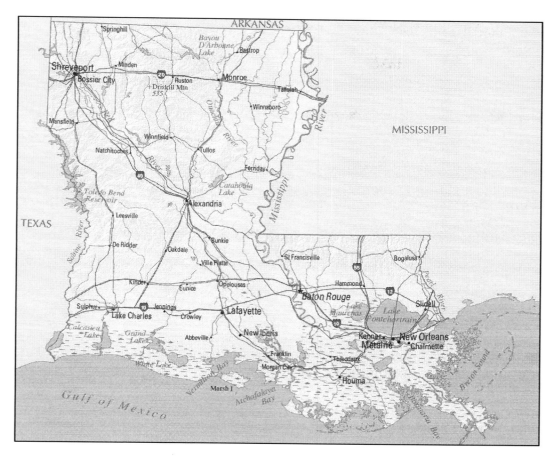

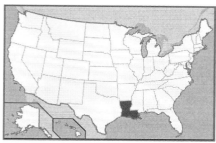

873. Which state borders Louisiana in the north?
     Arkansas
874. Which state borders Louisiana in the east?
     Mississippi
875. Which state borders Louisiana in the west?
     Texas
876. Which rivers make up the eastern boundary of Louisiana?
     Mississippi River and Pearl River
877. Which rivers make up part of the western boundary of Louisiana?
     Sabine River

878. Which water body lies to the south of Louisiana?
Gulf of Mexico

879. What are the nicknames of Louisiana?
Sportsman's Paradise; Pelican State; Bayou State; Child of the Mississippi; Creole State; Sugar State

880. What is the state motto of Louisiana?
Union, Justice, and Confidence

881. What are the state songs of Louisiana?
Give Me Louisiana; You Are My Sunshine

882. What is the state tree of Louisiana?
Bald Cypress

883. What is the state flower of Louisiana?
Magnolia Blossom

884. What is the state wildflower of Louisiana?
Louisiana Iris

885. What is the state bird of Louisiana?
Eastern Brown Pelican

886. What is the state dog of Louisiana?
Catahoula Leopard Dog

887. What is the state mammal of Louisiana?
Louisiana Black Bear

888. What is the state reptile of Louisiana?
Alligator

889. What is the state insect of Louisiana?
Honeybee

890. What is the state crustacean of Louisiana?
Crawfish

891. What is the state amphibian of Louisiana?
Green Tree Frog

892. What is the state freshwater fish of Louisiana?
White Perch

893. What is the state fossil of Louisiana?
Petrified Palmwood

894. What is the state gemstone of Louisiana?
Agate

895. What is the state beverage of Louisiana?
Milk

896. What are the state colors of Louisiana?
Blue, White and Gold

897. What is the state musical instrument of Louisiana?
Diatonic Accordion

898. What is the capital of Louisiana?
Baton Rouge

899. What is the largest city by population and area in Louisiana?
New Orleans

900. Who reached the mouth of Mississippi River in 1519?
    Alonso de Pineda (Spanish explorer)
901. Who explored Louisiana in 1542?
    Hernando de Soto (Spanish explorer)
902. Who navigated the Mississippi River and claimed for France all lands drained by the river and its tributaries, including Louisiana, in 1682?
    Robert de LaSalle (French explorer)
903. Robert de LaSalle named the Mississippi River area "La Louisiane" in honor of whom?
    King Louis XIV
904. Which city in Louisiana was the oldest permanent European settlement in the Louisiana Purchase territory, founded in 1714?
    Natchitoches
905. Which country controlled Louisiana in 1763 after the Treaty of Paris?
    Spain
906. In which year did Spain cede Louisiana back to France after the Treaty of San Ildefonso?
    1800
907. Louisiana west of the Mississippi River was purchased from France by which treaty signed on April 30th, 1803?
    Louisiana Purchase
908. When was the Territory of Orleans established?
    October 1st, 1804
909. When was Louisiana admitted to the Union?
    April 30th, 1812 (18th)
910. During which period did Louisiana secede from the Union?
    1861 – 1868
911. What is the area of Louisiana?
    51,843 sq mi / 135,382 km^2 (31st)
912. What is the population of Louisiana?
    4,649,676 (by 2014)
913. What is the topography of Louisiana?
    Uplands in the north; alluvial region along the coast; southern coast is among the fastest disappearing areas in the world
914. What is the highest point of Louisiana, located in the Appalachian Mountains?
    Driskill Mountain (535 ft / 163 m)
915. What is the lowest point of Louisiana?
    New Orleans (-7 ft / -2 m)
916. How long is the coastline of Louisiana?
    397 mi / 639 km (5th)
917. What are the major rivers in Louisiana?
    Mississippi River, Red River, Ouachita River, Atchafalaya River, and Sabine River
918. What are the major lakes in Louisiana?
    Lake Pontchartrain, Lake Maurepas, Toledo Bend Reservoir, Grand Lake, White Lake, Calcasieu Lake, and Catahoula Lake
919. Which city in Louisiana held first Mardi Gras parade in 1837?
    New Orleans

920. The first oil well and oil field in Louisiana were found in which city in 1901?
Jennings
921. What are nicknames of Jennings?
Garden Spot of Louisiana; Northern Town on Southern Soil
922. The first natural gas in Louisiana was found in which city in 1916?
Monroe
923. In which year was the first offshore oil well in Louisiana established?
1947
924. Which bridge in Louisiana was the longest over-water bridge in the world until 2011?
Lake Pontchartrain Causeway (24 mi / 38 km)
925. The Superdome, the world's largest steel-constructed room unobstructed by posts, was completed in which city of Louisiana in 1975?
New Orleans
926. The Louisiana State Capitol building, the tallest state capitol building in the United States (450 ft / 137 m, 34 floors), is located in which city?
Baton Rouge
927. Louisiana is the only state that does not have counties. What are the administrative subdivisions are called in Louisiana?
Parishes
928. Which basin in Saint Martin Parish of Louisiana is the largest swamp in the United States?
Atchafalaya Basin (930 sq mi / 2,410 km^2)
929. Which city in Louisiana is known as the Crawfish Capital of the World?
Breaux Bridge
930. Which city in Louisiana is known as the Stars and Stripes Capital of Louisiana?
Winnsboro
931. Which city in Louisiana is known as the Frog Capital of the World?
Rayne
932. Which town in Louisiana was once a hideaway for pirates?
Jean Lafitte (also the name of the famous pirate)
933. Which town in Louisiana is known as the Cajun Music Capital of the World?
Mamou
934. When did Hurricane Katrina strike southeastern Louisiana, causing more than 1,500 people killed and over 2 million homeless?
August 29th, 2005
935. What is the climate in Louisiana?
Humid subtropical
936. What are the natural resources in Louisiana?
Fertile soils, abundant deposits of oil and gas, and thick forests
937. What are the natural hazards in Louisiana?
Hurricanes, floods, and tornadoes
938. What are the major industries in Louisiana?
Agriculture (rice, cotton, soybeans), salt production, oil and natural gas, fishing (especially shellfish)

Maine

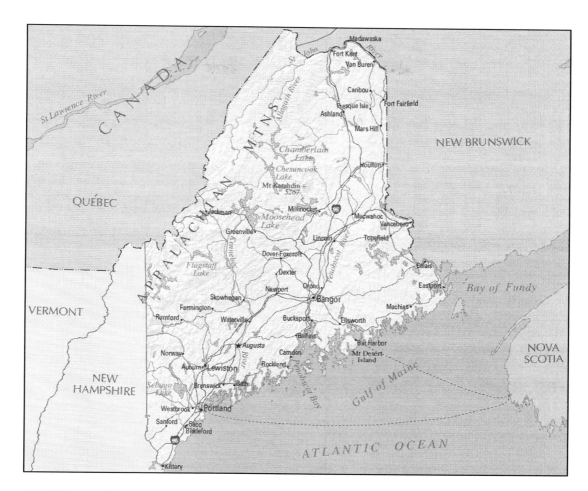

939. Which state borders Maine in the west?
New Hampshire
940. Which country borders Maine in the east, north and northwest?
Canada
941. Which water body lies to the south and east of Maine?
Atlantic Ocean
942. What is the nickname of Maine?
Pine Tree State
943. What is the state motto of Maine?

I Direct

944. What is the state song of Maine?
State of Maine Song
945. What is the state tree of Maine?
Eastern White Pine
946. What is the state flower of Maine?
White Pine Cone and Tassel
947. What is the state herb of Maine?
Wintergreen
948. What is the state berry of Maine?
Wild Blueberry
949. What is the state bird of Maine?
Black-capped Chickadee
950. What is the state animal of Maine?
Moose
951. What is the state insect of Maine?
Honeybee
952. What is the state cat of Maine?
Maine Coon Cat
953. What is the state fish of Maine?
Landlocked Salmon
954. What is the state fossil of Maine?
Pertica Quadrifaria
955. What is the state gemstone of Maine?
Tourmaline
956. What is the state soil of Maine?
Chesuncook Soil Series
957. What is the capital of Maine?
Augusta (the largest city by area)
958. What is the largest city by population in Maine?
Portland
959. Who explored the coast of Maine in 1498?
John Cabot (Italian navigator and explorer)
960. Who explored the coast of Maine in 1524?
Esteban Gómez (Portuguese cartographer and explorer)
961. Which island became the first European (French) settlement in Maine, founded in 1604?
St. Croix Island (also called Dochet Island)
962. Which island became the first permanent European (French and British) settlement in Maine, founded in 1622?
Monhegan Island
963. Which British colony, established on August 10th, 1622, included the present-day Maine, New Hampshire, Vermont, Quebec (Canada) and New Brunswick (Canada)?
Province of Maine
964. The Province of Maine became part of which colony in 1650s?
Massachusetts Bay Colony

965. District of Maine was part of which state until Maine became a separate state?
Massachusetts
966. When was Maine admitted to the Union?
March 15th, 1820 (23rd)
967. What is the area of Maine?
35,385 sq mi / 91,646 km^2 (39th)
968. What is the population of Maine?
1,330,089 (by 2014)
969. What is the topography of Maine?
Coastal lowlands in the southeast; Appalachian Mountains in the west; fjords in the south
970. What is the highest point of Maine, located in the Appalachian Mountains?
Mount Katahdin (5,268 ft / 1,606 m)
971. What is the lowest point of Maine?
Atlantic Ocean (0 ft / 0 m)
972. How long is the coastline of Maine?
228 mi / 367 km (9th)
973. What are the major rivers in Maine?
Androscoggin River, Kennebec River, Penobscot River, and St. John River
974. What are the major lakes in Maine?
Lake Moosehead and Richardson Lakes
975. Which national park is located in Maine?
Acadia National Park (74 sq mi / 192 km^2)
976. What is the Acadia National Park famous for?
Mountains, granite peaks, ocean shoreline, woodlands, and lakes on Mount Desert Island and other coastal islands
977. Which city in Maine is known as the City of Ships?
Bath
978. Which town in Maine is the nation's first chartered city?
York (1642)
979. Approximately what percent of the nation's lobster supply is caught off the coast of Maine?
90%
980. Approximately what percent of the nation's blueberries are produced in Maine?
99%
981. What is the climate in Maine?
Humid continental
982. What are the natural resources in Maine?
Vast forests and fertile soils
983. What are the natural hazards in Maine?
Hurricanes and winter storms
984. What are the major industries in Maine?
Agriculture (especially potatoes), ship building, fishing (especially lobsters), footwear, machinery, electronics, and tourism

Maryland

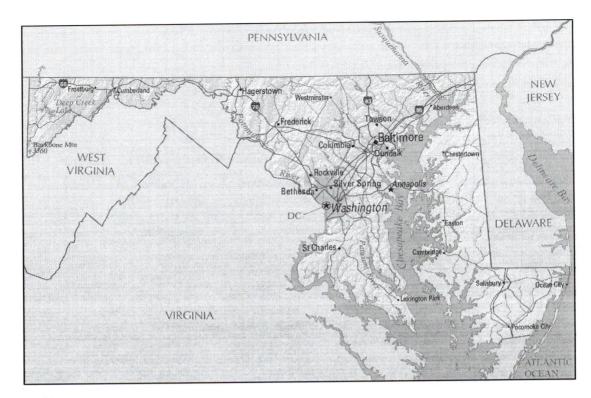

985. Which state borders Maryland in the north?
    Pennsylvania
986. Which state borders Maryland in the east?
    Delaware
987. Which state borders Maryland in the south and west?
    West Virginia
988. Which state borders Maryland in the south?
    Virginia
989. District of Columbia is between Maryland and which other state?
    Virginia
990. Which river makes up part of the southern boundary of Maryland?
    Potomac River
991. Which water body lies to the east of Maryland?
    Atlantic Ocean

992. Which water body nearly bisects Maryland?
Chesapeake Bay
993. What are the nicknames of Maryland?
Old Line State; Free State; Little America; America in Miniature
994. What is the state motto of Maryland?
Manly Deeds, Womanly Words
995. What is the state song of Maryland?
Maryland, My Maryland
996. What is the state tree of Maryland?
White Oak
997. What is the state flower of Maryland?
Black-eyed Susan
998. What is the state bird of Maryland?
Baltimore Oriole
999. What is the state reptile of Maryland?
Diamondback Terrapin
1000. What is the state fish of Maryland?
Rockfish
1001. What is the state crustacean of Maryland?
Maryland Blue Crab
1002. What is the state insect of Maryland?
Baltimore Checkerspot Butterfly
1003. What is the state dinosaur of Maryland?
Astrodon Johnston
1004. What is the state fossil shell of Maryland?
Ecphora Gardnerae Gardnerae
1005. What is the state dog of Maryland?
Chesapeake Bay Retriever
1006. What is the state beverage of Maryland?
Milk
1007. What is the state boat of Maryland?
Skipjack
1008. What is the state folk dance of Maryland?
Square Dance
1009. What is the state sport of Maryland?
Jousting
1010. What is the capital of Maryland?
Annapolis
1011. What is the largest city by population and area in Maryland?
Baltimore
1012. Who explored Maryland in 1608?
John Smith (British captain)
1013. Who established a trading post in 1622 on Kent Island, which became the first permanent European settlement in Maryland?
William Claiborne (British pioneer and surveyor)

1014. In which year was Province of Maryland, a British colony, established?
1632

1015. In which year did Maryland declare independence from Britain?
1776

1016. When was Maryland admitted to the Union?
April 28th, 1788 (7th)

1017. What is the area of Maryland?
12,407 sq mi / 32,133 km^2 (42nd)

1018. What is the population of Maryland?
5,976,407 (by 2014)

1019. What is the topography of Maryland?
Sandy dunes dotted with seagrass in the east; low marshlands teeming with wildlife and large bald cypress near the bay; gently rolling hills of oak forest in the Piedmont Region; pine groves in the mountains to the west

1020. What is the highest point of Maryland, a summit along the Backbone Mountain located in the Allegheny Mountains?
Hoye-Crest (3,360 ft / 1,020 m)

1021. What is the lowest point of Maryland?
Bloody Point Hole (-174 ft / -53 m)

1022. How long is the coastline of Maryland?
31 mi / 85 km (21st)

1023. What are the major rivers in Maryland?
Potomac River, Patapsco River, Patuxent River, and Susquehanna River

1024. What are the major lakes in Maryland?
Lake Oakland, Deep Creek Lake, Prettyboy Reservoir, and Loch Raven Reservoir

1025. Which city in Maryland was the temporary capital of the United States during 1783 – 1784?
Annapolis

1026. In which city of Maryland did King Williams School, the first school in the United States, opened in 1696 and became St. John's College in 1784?
Annapolis

1027. When did Francis Scott Key write the United States' national anthem, Star Spangled Banner, while watching the bombardment of Fort McHenry in Baltimore Harbor?
September 14th, 1814

1028. In which city of Maryland was the Basilica of the Assumption of the Blessed Virgin Mary, the first cathedral in the United States, built in 1821?
Baltimore

1029. In which city of Maryland was the United States Naval Academy founded on October 10th, 1845?
Annapolis

1030. In which city of Maryland was the Francis Scott Key Bridge (1,232 ft / 376 m), the 2nd longest continuous truss bridge in the United States, built in 1977?
Baltimore

1031. Which city in Maryland is known as the Sailing Capital of the World?
Annapolis

1032. Which city in Maryland is known as the Decoy Capitol of the World?

Havre de Grace

1033. Which city in Maryland was the first community in the United States built as a planned city and settled in 1937?
Greenbelt

1034. Which island in the Chesapeake Bay is Maryland's only inhabited off-shore island?
Smith Island

1035. What is the climate in Maryland?
Humid subtropical in the east; between humid subtropical and subtropical highland in the Piedmont Region; subtropical highland in the extreme west

1036. What are the natural resources in Maryland?
Fertile soils, sand, gravel deposits as well as clays, coal, limestone, and natural gas

1037. What are the natural hazards in Maryland?
Hurricanes, tornados, and winter storms

1038. What are the major industries in Maryland?
Farming (corn, soybeans, tobacco, poultry and dairy products), mining (coal), steel products, communications equipment, fishing (crabs and oysters), and government services

Massachusetts

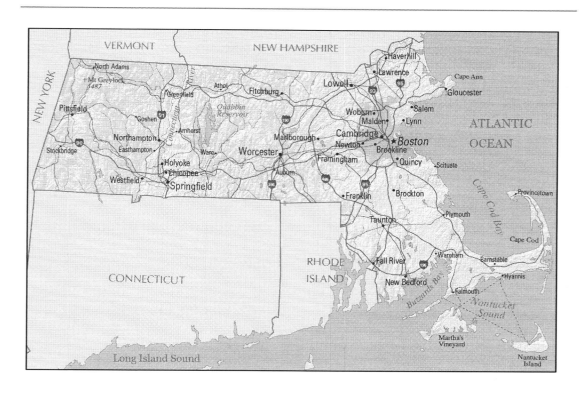

1039. Which states border Massachusetts in the north?
Vermont and New Hampshire
1040. Which states border Massachusetts in the south?
Rhode Island and Connecticut
1041. Which state borders Massachusetts in the west?
New York
1042. Which water body lies to the east of Massachusetts?
Atlantic Ocean
1043. What is the nickname of Massachusetts?
Bay State
1044. What is the state motto of Massachusetts?
By the Sword We Seek Peace, but Peace Only Under Liberty
1045. What is the state song of Massachusetts?
All Hail to Massachusetts
1046. What is the state tree of Massachusetts?
American Elm
1047. What is the state flower of Massachusetts?
Mayflower
1048. What is the state bean of Massachusetts?
Navy Bean
1049. What is the state bird of Massachusetts?
Black-Capped Chickadee
1050. What is the state game bird of Massachusetts?
Wild Turkey
1051. What is the state dog of Massachusetts?
Boston Terrier
1052. What is the state horse of Massachusetts?
Morgan Horse
1053. What is the state cat of Massachusetts?
Tabby Cat
1054. What is the state fish of Massachusetts?
Cod
1055. What is the state insect of Massachusetts?
Ladybug
1056. What is the state shell of Massachusetts?
New England Neptune

1057. What is the state marine mammal of Massachusetts?
Right Whale

1058. What is the state fossil of Massachusetts?
Dinosaur (Theropod) Tracks

1059. What is the state gem of Massachusetts?
Rhodonite

1060. What is the state mineral of Massachusetts?
Babingtonite

1061. What is the state rock of Massachusetts?
Roxbury Puddingstone

1062. What is the state historic rock of Massachusetts?
Plymouth Rock

1063. What is the state building rock of Massachusetts?
Granite

1064. What is the state explorer rock of Massachusetts?
Dighton Rock

1065. What is the state soil of Massachusetts?
Paxton Soil Series

1066. What is the state heroine of Massachusetts?
Deborah Samson

1067. What is the state folk hero of Massachusetts?
Johnny Appleseed

1068. What is the state folk dance of Massachusetts?
Square Dance

1069. What is the state polka of Massachusetts?
Say Hello to Someone from Massachusetts

1070. What is the state beverage of Massachusetts?
Cranberry Juice

1071. What is the state muffin of Massachusetts?
Corn Muffin

1072. What is the state dessert of Massachusetts?
Boston Cream Pie

1073. What is the state cookie of Massachusetts?
Chocolate Chip Cookie

1074. What is the capital of Massachusetts?
Boston (the largest city by population and area)

1075. When did the Mayflower crew first see Cape Cod?
November 9th, 1620

1076. When did the pilgrims first land at Plymouth, the 2nd oldest permanent English settlement in North America and the 4th oldest continuously inhabited city in the United States?
December 21st, 1620

1077. Plymouth was the first settlement in which British colony?
Plymouth Colony

1078. Which British colony existed around the present-day cities of Salem and Boston during 1628 – 1691?

Massachusetts Bay Colony

1079. What were the Salem Witch Trials in 1692?
Hundreds people were accused and jailed by their fellow townspeople for being witches, and 20 men and women were executed

1080. What was the Boston Massacre (also called the Boston Riot) on March 5th, 1770?
An incident in which British redcoats killed 5 civilian men

1081. What was the Boston Tea Party on December 16th, 1773?
Being angered by taxation from British Parliament, colonists boarded three ships in Boston Harbor and tossed the cargoes of tea into the water

1082. The Boston Massacre and Boston Tea Party led to which war during April 19th, 1775 – September 3rd, 1783?
American Revolutionary War

1083. Which British colony, established on October 7th, 1691, included the Massachusetts Bay Colony, Plymouth Colony, the Province of Maine, Martha's Vineyard, Nantucket, Nova Scotia (Canada) and New Brunswick (Canada)?
Province of Massachusetts Bay

1084. When was Massachusetts admitted to the Union?
February 6th, 1788 (6th)

1085. What is the area of Massachusetts?
10,555 sq mi / 27,336 km^2 (44th)

1086. What is the population of Massachusetts?
6,745,408 (by 2014)

1087. What is the topography of Massachusetts?
Berkshire Mountains in the far west; Pioneer Valley in the west; deeply indented coastline in the southeast, with bays, coves, and estuaries, separated by narrow promontories; Cape Cod is the largest promontory; largest islands: Martha's Vineyard, Nantucket, the Elizabeth Islands, and Monomoy Island

1088. What is the highest point of Massachusetts, located in the Taconic Mountains?
Mount Greylock (3,489 ft / 1,063 m)

1089. What is the lowest point of Massachusetts?
Atlantic Ocean (0 ft / 0 m)

1090. How long is the coastline of Massachusetts?
192 mi / 309 km (10th)

1091. What are the major rivers in Massachusetts?
Charles River, Connecticut River, and Merrimack River

1092. What is the major lake in Massachusetts?
Quabbin Reservoir

1093. The first Thanksgiving Day was celebrated in which town in Massachusetts in 1621?
Plymouth

1094. Boston Common, the oldest city park in the United States built in 1634, is located in which city of Massachusetts?
Boston

1095. What is the oldest public school with a continuous existence in the United States, founded on April 23rd, 1635?
Boston Latin School

1096. What is the oldest institution of higher learning in the United States, founded by the General Court on October 28th, 1636?
Harvard College (one of two schools within Harvard University)
1097. The Mather school was founded in Dorchester of which city in 1639 as the first public elementary school in the United States?
Boston
1098. Mount Holyoke Seminary, America's first college for women, was built in which town of Massachusetts in 1837?
South Hadley
1099. Elias Howe, resident of which city in Massachusetts, invented the first sewing machine in 1845?
Boston
1100. The first subway system in the United States was built in which city of Massachusetts in 1897?
Boston
1101. The newspaper house was built in which town of Massachusetts during 1922 – 1924?
Rockport
1102. The birth control pill was invented at Clark University, located in which city of Massachusetts?
Worcester
1103. Revere Beach, located in which city of Massachusetts, was the first public beach in the United States?
Revere
1104. Which city in Massachusetts is known as the Cradle of the American Industrial Revolution?
Lowell
1105. Which town in Massachusetts is known as the Wedding Capital of Cape Cod?
Brewster
1106. What is the climate in Massachusetts?
Humid continental
1107. What are the natural resources in Massachusetts?
Fertile Connecticut River Valley soils, most rich in peat, deposits of sand and gravel, glacial stones and boulders (granite, marble)
1108. What are the natural hazards in Massachusetts?
Hurricanes, tornados, and winter storms
1109. What are the major industries in Massachusetts?
Textiles, electronics, publishing, education, tourism, and fishing

Michigan

1110. Which states border Michigan in the south?
Indiana and Ohio
1111. Which state border Michigan in the west?
Wisconsin

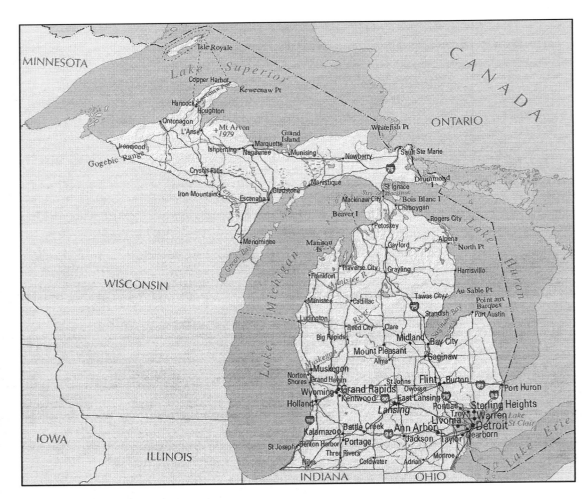

1112. Which state lies to the west of Michigan, across Lake Michigan?
Illinois

1113. Which state lies to the west of Michigan, across Lake Superior?
Minnesota

1114. Which country borders Michigan in the north and east?
Canada

1115. Which great lakes border Michigan?
Lake Erie, Lake Huron, Lake Michigan, and Lake Superior

1116. The Soo Canal and Locks connect which two lakes?
    Lake Superior and Lake Huron
1117. Which river drains Lake Superior into Lake Huron?
    St. Mary's River
1118. Which major islands of Michigan are located in Lake Michigan?
    North Manitou, South Manitou, Beaver, and Fox Islands
1119. Which major islands of Michigan are located in Lake Superior?
    Isle Royale and Grande Isle
1120. Which major islands of Michigan are located in Lake Huron?
    Marquette, Bois Blanc, and Mackinac Island
1121. Which major islands of Michigan are located in St. Mary's River?
    Neebish, Sugar, and Drummond islands
1122. What are the nicknames of Michigan?
    Great Lakes State; Wolverine State
1123. What is the state motto of Michigan?
    If You Seek a Pleasant Peninsula, Look Around You
1124. What is the state song of Michigan?
    Michigan, My Michigan
1125. What is the state tree of Michigan?
    White Pine
1126. What is the state flower of Michigan?
    Apple Blossom
1127. What is the state wildflower of Michigan?
    Dwarf Lake Iris
1128. What is the state bird of Michigan?
    Robin
1129. What is the state stone of Michigan?
    Petoskey Stone
1130. What is the state gem of Michigan?
    Chlorastrolite (Michigan Greenstone)
1131. What is the state soil of Michigan?
    Kalkaska Sand
1132. What is the capital of Michigan?
    Lansing
1133. What is the largest city by population and area in Michigan?
    Detroit
1134. Who explored Michigan in 1620?
    Étienne Brûlé (French explorer)
1135. The first European (French) settlement in Michigan was founded in which city by Jacques Marquette (French explorer) in 1668?
    Sault Ste. Marie
1136. Who founded a trading post on the Detroit River in 1701, which became the present-day Detroit?
    Antoine de Lamothe Cadillac (French explorer and adventurer)
1137. Which country captured Detroit in 1760, ending

British

1138. When was the Territory of Michigan established?
June 30th, 1805

1139. When was Michigan admitted to the Union?
January 26th, 1837 (26th)

1140. What is the area of Michigan?
96,716 sq mi / 250,493 km^2 (11th)

1141. What is the population of Michigan?
9,909,877 (by 2014)

1142. What is the topography of Michigan?
Upper Peninsula and Lower Peninsula, separated by the Straits of Mackinac; Porcupine Mountains in the west of the Upper Peninsula; plains in the Lower Peninsula

1143. What is the highest point of Michigan, located in the Huron Mountains?
Mount Arvon (1,979 ft / 603 m)

1144. What is the lowest point of Michigan?
Lake Erie (571 ft / 174 m)

1145. What are the major rivers in Michigan?
Detroit River, Grand River, Kalamazoo River, St. Clair River, and St. Mary's River

1146. What are the major lakes in Michigan?
Lake Michigan, Lake Superior, Lake Huron, Lake Erie, and Lake St. Clair

1147. Which national park is located in Michigan?
Isle Royale National Park (831 sq mi / 2,314 km^2)

1148. What is Isle Royale National Park famous for?
Many shipwrecks, waterways, and hiking trails

1149. Which university in Michigan was the first university established by a state in 1817?
University of Michigan (originally named Cathelepistemian)

1150. Which city in Michigan is known as the Cereal Capital of the World?
Battle Creek

1151. Which city in Michigan is known as the Car Capital of the World?
Detroit

1152. Ransom Eli Olds founded the Olds Motor Vehicle Company in which city of Michigan on August 21st, 1897?
Lansing

1153. The Olds Motor Vehicle Company was bought by a copper and lumber magnate named Samuel L. Smith in 1899, renamed to Olds Motor Works, and relocated to which city in Michigan?
Detroit

1154. The Ford Motor Company was founded by Henry Ford, and incorporated in which city of Michigan on June 16th, 1903?
Dearborn (a suburb of Detroit)

1155. The General Motors was founded in which city of Michigan on September 16th, 1908?
Flint (northwest of Detroit)

1156. United Auto Workers (UAW), a labor union found in May 1935, is headquartered in which city of Michigan?
Detroit

1157. What is the longest suspension bridge in the United States, spanning the Straits of Mackinac to connect the non-contiguous Upper and Lower peninsulas of Michigan?
The Mackinac Bridge (also called the Big Mac and the Mighty Mac, 26,372 ft / 8,038 m)

1158. Which suspension bridge in Michigan connects Detroit and Windsor (Canada)?
Ambassador Bridge

1159. What is the first auto traffic tunnel between two nations, built in 1930?
Detroit-Windsor tunnel

1160. The world's first international submarine railway tunnel was opened between which city in Michigan and Sarnia (Canada) in 1891?
Port Huron

1161. What is the climate in Michigan?
Continental (the southern and central parts of the Lower Peninsula have a warmer climate than the northern part of Lower Peninsula and the entire Upper Peninsula)

1162. What are the natural resources in Michigan?
Fertile soils, rich mineral deposits (iron ore, copper, petroleum, natural gas, salt, limestone, shale, gypsum, sand and gravel), widespread forests, plentiful water, and abundant plant and animal life

1163. What are the natural hazards in Michigan?
Hurricanes, tornados, wildfires, and winter storms

1164. What are the major industries in Michigan?
Car manufacturing, farming (corn, soybeans, wheat), timber, and fishing

Minnesota

1165. Which states border Minnesota in the west?
North Dakota and South Dakota

1166. Which state borders Minnesota in the south?
Iowa

1167. Which state borders Minnesota in the east?
Wisconsin

1168. Which country borders Minnesota in the north?
Canada

1169. Which state lies to the east of Minnesota, across Lake Superior?
Michigan

1170. Which rivers make up part of the eastern boundary of Minnesota?
Mississippi River and St. Croix River

1171. Which rivers make up part of the western boundary of Minnesota?
Red River and Minnesota River

1172. Which water body lies to the east of Minnesota?
Lake Superior

1173. What are the nicknames of Minnesota?
North Star State; Land of 10,000 Lakes; Gopher State

1174. What is the state motto of Minnesota?
The Star of the North

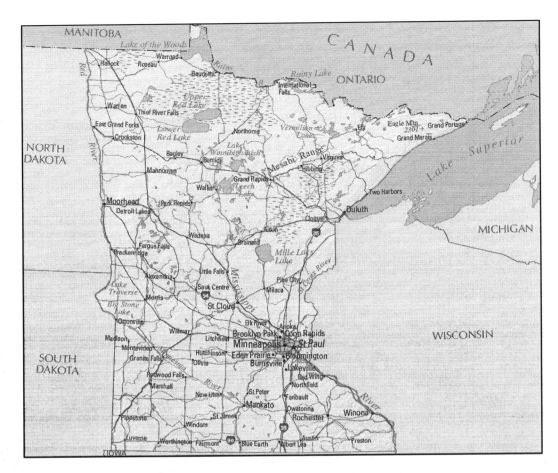

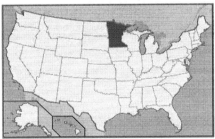

1175. What is the state song of Minnesota?
Hail Minnesota

1176. What is the state tree of Minnesota?
Norway Pine

1177. What is the state flower of Minnesota?
Pink and White Lady's Slipper

1178. What is the state bird of Minnesota?
Common Loon

1179. What is the state mushroom of Minnesota?
Morel

1180. What is the state grain of Minnesota?
Wild Rice

1181. What is the state insect of Minnesota?
Monarch Butterfly

1182. What is the state fish of Minnesota?
Walleye

1183. What is the state gemstone of Minnesota?
Lake Superior Agate

1184. What is the state beverage of Minnesota?
Milk

1185. What is the state muffin of Minnesota?
Blueberry

1186. What is the capital of Minnesota?
Saint Paul

1187. What is the largest city by population in Minnesota?
Minneapolis

1188. What is the largest city by area in Minnesota?
Duluth

1189. What are twin cities in Minnesota?
Minneapolis and Saint Paul

1190. Who explored the western end of Lake Superior and the surrounding area in 1659?
Groseilliers and Radisson (French fur traders)

1191. Who explored Minnesota in 1673?
Jacques Marquette (French explorer) and Louis Jolliet (French missionary)

1192. Which country received Louisiana Territory, including Minnesota west of the Mississippi River, from France in 1763?
Spain

1193. The United States took control of eastern portion of Minnesota from whom in 1783?
British

1194. Western portion of Minnesota was purchased from France by which treaty signed on April 30th, 1803?
Louisiana Purchase

1195. Which city is the oldest in Minnesota that has been occupied continuously since 1826?
Wabasha

1196. Minnesota became part of which territory on July 3rd, 1836?
Territory of Wisconsin

1197. When was the Territory of Iowa (including Minnesota) established, split from the Territory of Wisconsin?
July 4th, 1838

1198. When was the Territory of Minnesota established, split from the Territory of Iowa?
March 3rd, 1849

1199. When was Minnesota admitted to the Union?
May 11th, 1858 (32nd)

1200. What is the area of Minnesota?
86,939 sq mi / 225,181 km^2 (12th)

1201. What is the population of Minnesota?
5,457,173 (by 2014)

1202. What is the topography of Minnesota?
Mostly flat; Messabi Range and Sawtooth Mountains in the northeast

1203. What is the highest point of Minnesota, located in the Misquah Hills?
Eagle Mountain (2,302 ft / 701 m)

1204. What is the lowest point of Minnesota?
Lake Superior (601 ft / 183 m)

1205. What are the major rivers in Minnesota?
Minnesota River, Mississippi River, Rainy River, Red River of the North, and St. Croix River

1206. What are the major lakes in Minnesota?
Upper Red Lake, Lower Red Lake, Mille Lacs Lake, Vermillion Lake, Rainy Lake, Lake of the Woods, Lake Superior, Leech Lake, Winnibigoshish Lake, and Lake Pepin

1207. Which national park is located in Minnesota?
Voyageurs National Park (341 sq mi / 883 km^2)

1208. What is Voyageurs National Park famous for?
Located on Rainy Lake, Kabetogama Lake, Namakan Lake, and Sand Point Lake, it is famous for canoeing, kayaking, and fishing; it has historic sites of Ojibwe Native Americans, French fur traders called voyageurs, and gold rush

1209. Which part of Minnesota, located in Lake of the Woods, is the only part of the 48 contiguous states lying north of the 49th Parallel?
Northwest Angle

1210. The Mall of America, located in which city of Minnesota, is the largest mall by the total enclosed floor area, and the 2nd largest in North America?
Bloomington

1211. The Old Log Theater, located in which city of Minnesota, claims to be the oldest continuously operating professional theater in the United States since 1940?
Minneapolis

1212. Which city in Minnesota claims to be the Lutefisk Capital of the World?
Madison

1213. Which city in Minnesota is the coldest city in the United States, measured by the average annual temperature?
International Falls (36 °F / 2 °C)

1214. What are the nicknames of International Falls?
Icebox of the Nation; Frostbite Falls

1215. What is the climate in Minnesota?
Continental

1216. What are the natural resources in Minnesota?
Fertile soil, minerals (iron ore, manganese, granite, limestone, sandstone), and forests

1217. What are the natural hazards in Minnesota?
Tornados, floods, winter storms, and wildfires

1218. What are the major industries in Minnesota?
Farming (corn, soybeans, sugar beets, wheat, dairy products), paper pulp, mining (iron ore)

Mississippi

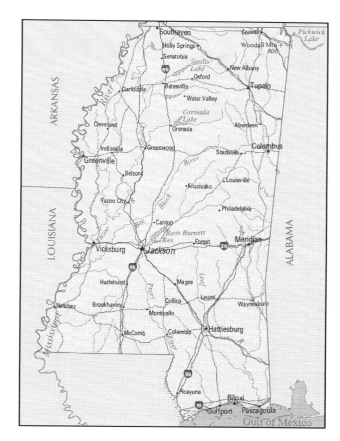

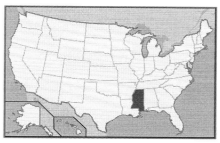

1219. Which state borders Mississippi in the north?
Tennessee

1220. Which state borders Mississippi in the east?
Alabama

1221. Which state borders Mississippi in the south and west?
Louisiana

1222. Which state borders Mississippi in the west?
Arkansas

1223. Which rivers make up the western boundary of Mississippi?
Mississippi River and Pearl River

1224. Which water body lies to the south of Mississippi?
Gulf of Mexico

1225. What are the nicknames of Mississippi?
Magnolia State; Hospitality State

1226. What is the state motto of Mississippi?
By Valor and Arms

1227. What is the state song of Mississippi?
Go Mis-sis-sip-pi

1228. What is the state tree of Mississippi?
Magnolia

1229. What is the state flower of Mississippi?
Magnolia
1230. What is the state bird of Mississippi?
Mockingbird
1231. What is the state game bird of Mississippi?
Wood Duck
1232. What is the state mammal of Mississippi?
White-tailed Deer
1233. What is the state water mammal of Mississippi?
Bottle-nosed Dolphin
1234. What is the state bird of Mississippi?
Honeybee
1235. What is the state shell of Mississippi?
Oyster
1236. What is the state fish of Mississippi?
Largemouth Bass
1237. What is the state butterfly of Mississippi?
Spicebush Swallowtail
1238. What is the state fossil of Mississippi?
Prehistoric Whale
1239. What is the state stone of Mississippi?
Petrified Wood
1240. What is the state beverage of Mississippi?
Milk
1241. What is the capital of Mississippi?
Jackson (the largest city by population and area)
1242. Who explored Mississippi in 1540?
Hernando de Soto (Spanish explorer)
1243. Who explored Mississippi in 1673?
Jacques Marquette (French explorer) and Louis Jolliet (French missionary)
1244. Who navigated the Mississippi River and claimed for France all lands drained by the river and its tributaries, including Mississippi, in 1682?
Robert de LaSalle (French explorer)
1245. Which fort became the first European (French) settlement in Mississippi, founded on May 1st, 1699?
Fort Maurepas (also called Old Biloxi)
1246. Which fort became the oldest European (French) permanent settlement along the Mississippi River, founded in 1716?
Fort Rosalie (the present-day Natchez)
1247. Who controlled Mississippi during 1763 – 1779?
British
1248. Who controlled Mississippi during 1779 – 1798?
Spanish
1249. When was the Territory of Mississippi established?
April 7th, 1798

1250. When was Mississippi admitted to the Union?
December 10th, 1817 (20th)

1251. During which period did Mississippi secede from the Union?
1861 – 1865

1252. What is the area of Mississippi?
48,430 sq mi / 125,443 km^2 (32nd)

1253. What is the population of Mississippi?
2,994,079 (by 2014)

1254. What is the topography of Mississippi?
East Gulf Coastal Plain in the center and east; Mississippi Alluvial Plain in the west

1255. What is the highest point of Mississippi, located in the Appalachian Mountains?
Woodall Mountain (807 ft / 246 m)

1256. What is the lowest point of Mississippi?
Gulf of Mexico (0 ft / 0 m)

1257. How long is the coastline of Mississippi?
44 mi / 71 km (19th)

1258. What are the major rivers in Mississippi?
Mississippi River, Big Black River, Pearl River, and Yazoo River

1259. What are the major lakes in Mississippi?
Ross Barnett Reservoir, Arkabutla Lake, Sardis Lake, and Grenada Lake

1260. The world's largest cactus plantation is located in which town of Mississippi?
Edwards

1261. Which town in Mississippi is called the Sweet Potato Capital of the World?
Vardaman

1262. The world's largest cottonwood tree plantation is located in which county of Mississippi?
Issaquena

1263. The International Checkers Hall of Fame is located in which city of Mississippi?
Petal

1264. The world's largest pecan nursery is located in which city of Mississippi?
Lumberton

1265. Which city in Mississippi is called the Cotton Capital of the World?
Greenwood

1266. Which city in Mississippi is called the Catfish Capital of the World?
Belzoni

1267. Which city in Mississippi is called the Towboat Capital of the World?
Greenville

1268. What is the climate in Mississippi?
Humid subtropical

1269. What are the natural resources in Mississippi?
Rich soils, abundant water, petroleum, natural gas, forests, and mineral resources

1270. What are the natural hazards in Mississippi?
Tornados and floods

1271. What are the major industries in Mississippi?
Farming (cotton, corn, soybeans, rice), oil, textiles, electronic equipment, transportation equipment, and fishing

Missouri

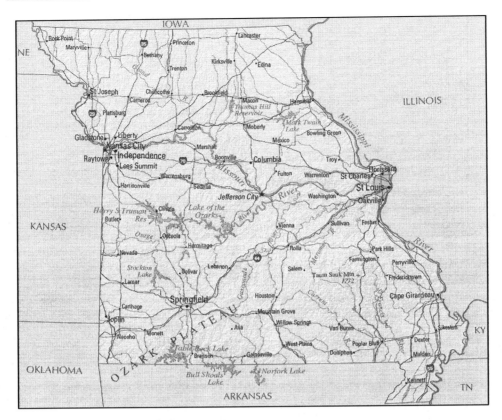

1272. Which state borders Missouri in the north?
      Iowa
1273. Which states border Missouri in the east?
      Illinois, Kentucky, and Tennessee
1274. Which state borders Missouri in the south?
      Arkansas
1275. Which states border Missouri in the west?
      Oklahoma, Kansas, and Nebraska
1276. Which river makes up part of the eastern boundary of Missouri?

Mississippi River

1277. Which river makes up part of the western boundary of Missouri?
Missouri River

1278. What is the nickname of Missouri?
Show-Me State

1279. What is the state motto of Missouri?
The Welfare of the People Shall Be the Supreme Law

1280. What is the state song of Missouri?
Missouri Waltz

1281. What is the state tree of Missouri?
Flowering Dogwood

1282. What is the state nut tree of Missouri?
Eastern Black Walnut Tree

1283. What is the state flower of Missouri?
White Hawthorn

1284. What is the state bird of Missouri?
Bluebird

1285. What is the state animal of Missouri?
Missouri Mule

1286. What is the state insect of Missouri?
Honeybee

1287. What is the state aquatic animal of Missouri?
Paddlefish

1288. What is the state fish of Missouri?
Channel Catfish

1289. What is the state fossil of Missouri?
Crinoid

1290. What is the state mineral of Missouri?
Galena

1291. What is the state rock of Missouri?
Mozarkite

1292. What is the state musical instrument of Missouri?
Fiddle

1293. What is the state folk dance of Missouri?
Square Dance

1294. What is the capital of Missouri?
Jefferson City

1295. What is the largest city by population and area in Missouri?
Kansas City

1296. Who explored Missouri in 1673?
Jacques Marquette (French explorer) and Louis Jolliet (French missionary)

1297. Who navigated the Mississippi River and claimed for France all lands drained by the river and its tributaries, including Missouri, in 1682?
Robert de LaSalle (French explorer)

1298. Which country received Louisiana Territory, including Missouri, from France in 1763?

Spain

1299. Pierre Laclède Liguest (French fur trader) and his assistant, Rene Auguste Chouteau (American fur trader and politician), founded which city of Missouri in 1764?
St. Louis

1300. In which year was Missouri returned to France by Spain?
1800

1301. Missouri was purchased from France by which treaty signed on April 30th, 1803?
Louisiana Purchase

1302. The Lewis and Clark Expedition started from which city of Missouri in 1804?
St. Louis

1303. When was the Territory of Missouri established?
June 4th, 1812

1304. When was Missouri admitted to the Union?
August 10th, 1821 (24th)

1305. What is the area of Missouri?
69,704 sq mi / 180,533 km^2 (21st)

1306. What is the population of Missouri?
6,063,589 (by 2014)

1307. What is the topography of Missouri?
Northern Plains in the north; Ozark Plateau in the south

1308. What is the highest point of Missouri, located in the Saint Francois Mountains?
Taum Sauk Mountain (1,772 ft / 540 m)

1309. What is the lowest point of Missouri?
Saint Francis River at southern Arkansas border (230 ft / 70 m)

1310. What are the major rivers in Missouri?
Mississippi River, Missouri River, and Osage River

1311. What are the major lakes in Missouri?
Lake of the Ozarks, Table Rock Lake, Clearwater Lake, and Lake Wappapello

1312. Which city in Missouri has more miles of boulevards than Paris and more fountains than any city except Rome?
Kansas City

1313. The Gateway Arch, the tallest man-made monument in the United States (630 ft / 192 m), is located in which city of Missouri?
St. Louis

1314. Anheuser-Busch InBev, the world's largest brewer, is located in which city of Missouri?
St. Louis

1315. What are nicknames of St. Louis?
Rome of the West; STL; Gateway to the West; Mound City; Home of the Blues

1316. Which city in Missouri was the primary starting point of the famed Oregon Trail, which led settlers to modern day Oregon?
Independence

1317. In which international fair in 1904 were the iced tea and ice cream cone invented?
St. Louis World's Fair

1318. What is the climate in Missouri?
Humid continental

1319. What are the natural resources in Missouri?

Fertile soils and large mineral (lead, copper, zinc, barite, limestone, dolomite, granite, marble, sandstone, coal) deposits

1320. What are the natural hazards in Missouri?

Tornados, hurricanes, earthquakes, and floods

1321. What are the major industries in Missouri?

Farming (corn, soybeans), mining (zinc, lead), aircraft equipment, cars, and beer

Montana

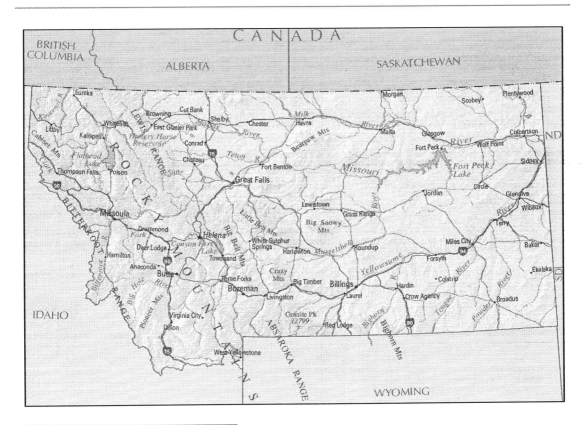

1322. Which states border Montana in the east?

North Dakota and South Dakota

1323. Which state borders Montana in the west and south?

Idaho
1324. Which state borders Montana in the south?
Wyoming
1325. Which country borders Montana in the north?
Canada
1326. What are the nicknames of Montana?
Big Sky Country; Treasure State
1327. What is the state motto of Montana?
Gold and Silver
1328. What is the state song of Montana?
Montana
1329. What is the state tree of Montana?
Ponderosa Pine
1330. What is the state flower of Montana?
Bitterroot
1331. What is the state grass of Montana?
Bluebunch Wheatgrass
1332. What is the state bird of Montana?
Western Meadowlark
1333. What is the state animal of Montana?
Grizzly Bear
1334. What is the state fish of Montana?
Cutthroat Trout
1335. What is the state fossil of Montana?
Maiasaura Peeblesorum
1336. What are the state gemstones of Montana?
Sapphire and Montana Agate
1337. What is the capital of Montana?
Helena
1338. What is the largest city by population in Montana?
Billings
1339. What is the largest city by area in Montana?
Butte
1340. In which year did two sons of Pierre Gaultier de Varennes (French Canadian military officer, fur trader, and explorer) discover Rocky Mountains?
1743
1341. Potion of Montana was purchased from France by which treaty signed on April 30th, 1803?
Louisiana Purchase
1342. Who found St. Mary's Mission in Bitteroot Valley, the first permanent European settlement in Montana, in 1841?
Pierre-Jean De Smet (Belgian priest)
1343. Which city was the first permanent fort in Montana, founded by Rene Auguste Chouteau (American fur trader and politician) and Pierre Chouteau, Jr. (American merchant) in 1847?
Fort Benton
1344. When was the Territory of Montana established, split from the Territory of Idaho?

May 28th, 1864

1345. When was Montana admitted to the Union?
November 8th, 1889 (41st)

1346. What is the area of Montana?
147,042 sq mi / 381,156 km^2 (4th)

1347. What is the population of Montana?
1,023,579 (by 2014)

1348. What is the topography of Montana?
Great Plains in the east; Rocky Mountains in the west

1349. What is the highest point of Montana, located in the Beartooth Mountains?
Granite Peak (12,807 ft / 3,903 m)

1350. What is the lowest point of Montana?
Kootenai River at Idaho border (1,804 ft / 550 m)

1351. What are the major rivers in Montana?
Yellowstone River, Missouri River, and Clark Fork River

1352. What are the major lakes in Montana?
Flathead Lake and Fort Peck Lake

1353. Which lake is the largest natural freshwater lake in the western part of the 48 contiguous United States?
Flathead Lake (191 sq mi / 496 km^2)

1354. Which national parks are located in Montana?
Glacier National Park (1,584 sq mi / 4,102 km^2) and Yellowstone National Park (in Wyoming, Montana, and Idaho, 3,472 sq mi / 8,987 km^2)

1355. What is Glacier National Park famous for?
26 remaining glaciers, 130 named lakes, and more than a hundred unnamed lakes under the tall Rocky Mountain peaks

1356. Where inside Glacier National Park does the Laurentian Divide meet the Great Divide?
Triple Divide Peak

1357. Glacier National Park and Waterton Lakes National Park (Canada) form which international park?
Waterton-Glacier International Peace Park

1358. Montana has the most different species of mammals in the United States. How many are they?
19 large mammal and 96 small mammal species

1359. What is the population order from most to least among elks, deer, antelopes, and humans in Montana?
Deer, antelopes, elks, and humans

1360. Approximately how many snow geese are in the Freezeout Lake during migration?
300,000

1361. Approximately how many white pelicans are in the Medicine Lake during migration?
10,000

1362. Which city in Montana is known as the Cowboy Capitol?
Miles City

1363. Which town was named for the daughter of the famous Sioux chief, Sitting Bull?
Ekalaka

1364. How many Indian reservations are located in Montana?
7
1365. What was discovered in 1977 by Marion Brandvold at the Egg Mountain?
Bones of juvenile dinosaurs
1366. The Roe River (201 ft / 61 m) in which city of Montana was listed as the shortest river in the Guinness World Records until the category was removed in 2006?
Great Falls
1367. What is the nickname of Great Falls?
Electric City
1368. What is the climate in Montana?
Semi-arid, continental climate in the east; coastal climate in the west
1369. What are the natural resources in Montana?
Mineral reserves, large areas of cropland, grassland, forested land, coal and petroleum reserves
1370. What are the natural hazards in Montana?
Earthquakes, wildfires, and blizzards
1371. What are the major industries in Montana?
Farming (wheat, sugar beets), cattle ranching, mining (gold, silver, copper, coal), oil, lumber, and tourism

Nebraska

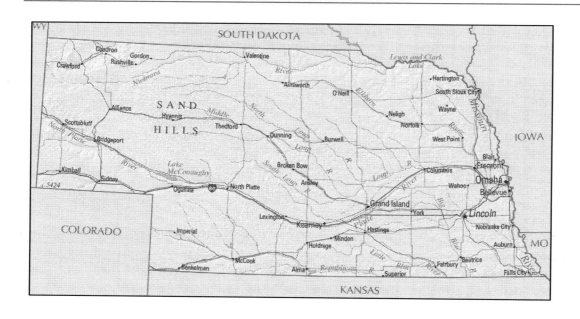

1372. Which state borders Nebraska in the north?
South Dakota

1373. Which states border Nebraska in the east?
Iowa and Missouri

1374. Which state borders Nebraska in the southwest?
Colorado

1375. Which state borders Nebraska in the south?
Kansas

1376. Which state borders Nebraska in the west?
Wyoming

1377. Which river makes up the eastern boundary of Nebraska?
Missouri River

1378. What is Nebraska Panhandle?
Western part of Nebraska, in the shape of a panhandle

1379. What are the nicknames of Nebraska?
Cornhusker State; Tree Planters' State

1380. What is the state motto of Nebraska?
Equality before the Law

1381. What is the state song of Nebraska?
Beautiful Nebraska

1382. What is the state tree of Nebraska?
Cottonwood

1383. What is the state flower of Nebraska?
Goldenrod

1384. What is the state grass of Nebraska?
Little Bluestem

1385. What is the state bird of Nebraska?
Western Meadowlark

1386. What is the state mammal of Nebraska?
White-tailed Deer

1387. What is the state fish of Nebraska?
Channel Catfish

1388. What is the state fossil of Nebraska?
Mammoth

1389. What is the state insect of Nebraska?
Honeybee

1390. What is the state rock of Nebraska?

Prairie Agate

1391. What is the state gemstone of Nebraska?

Blue Chalcedony

1392. What is the state soil of Nebraska?

Holdrege

1393. What is the state beverage of Nebraska?

Milk

1394. What is the state soft drink of Nebraska?

Kool-Aid

1395. What is the state river of Nebraska?

Platte River

1396. What is the state American folk dance of Nebraska?

Square Dance

1397. What is the capital of Nebraska?

Lincoln

1398. What is the largest city by population and area in Nebraska?

Omaha

1399. Who explored Kansas in 1541, and claimed the entire territory for Spain, including Nebraska?

Francisco Vásquez de Coronado (Spanish conquistador)

1400. Who navigated the Mississippi River and claimed for France all lands drained by the river and its tributaries, including Nebraska, in 1682?

Robert de LaSalle (French explorer)

1401. Nebraska was purchased from France by which treaty signed on April 30th, 1803?

Louisiana Purchase

1402. What was the first European settlement in Nebraska, founded by Manuel Lisa (Spanish fur trader) in 1812?

Fort Lisa

1403. What was the first permanent European settlement in Nebraska, founded by Joshua Pilcher (American fur trader) in 1822?

Bellevue

1404. When was the Territory of Nebraska established?

May 30th, 1854

1405. When was Nebraska admitted to the Union?

March 1st, 1867 (37th)

1406. What is the area of Nebraska?

77,354 sq mi / 200,520 km^2 (16th)

1407. What is the population of Nebraska?

1,881,503 (by 2014)

1408. What is the topography of Nebraska?

Dissected Till Plains in the east; Great Plains in the west; the state has more miles of river than any other state

1409. What is the highest point of Nebraska, near the point where Nebraska, Wyoming, and Colorado meet?

Panorama Point (5,427 ft / 1,654 m)

1410. What is the lowest point of Nebraska?
Missouri River at Kansas border (840 ft / 256 m)

1411. What are the major rivers in Nebraska?
Missouri River, Niobrara River, Platte River, and Republican River

1412. What are the major lakes in Nebraska?
Lewis and Clark Lake, Harlan County Lake, and Lake C.W. McConaughty

1413. What is the Chimney Rock in western Nebraska?
A prominent geological rock formation rising nearly 300 ft (91 m) above the surrounding North Platte River valley (elevation: 4,226 ft / 1,288 m), which served as a landmark along the Oregon Trail, the California Trail, and the Mormon Trail

1414. In which town of Nebraska did N.H. Darton first locate the Ogallala Aquifer (also called High Plains Aquifer) in 1898, a vast yet shallow underground water table aquifer located beneath the Great Plains in the United States, covering South Dakota, Nebraska, Wyoming, Colorado, Kansas, Oklahoma, New Mexico, and Texas (174,000 sq mi / 450,000 km²)?
Ogallala

1415. The Union Pacific's Bailey Yards, the largest rail classification complex in the world, is located in which city of Nebraska?
North Platte

1416. Kool-Aid was invented in which city of Nebraska by Edward Perkins in 1927?
Hastings

1417. The 911 system of emergency communications was developed and first used in which city of Nebraska?
Lincoln

1418. Which city in Nebraska has the United States' largest limestone deposit and is the largest limestone producer?
Weeping Water

1419. Which county in Nebraska is the origin of the world's largest Woolly Mammoth elephant fossil?
Lincoln

1420. Which counties in Nebraska are named after animals?
Antelope and Buffalo

1421. What is the largest hand-planted forest in the United States, located near Thedford, Nebraska?
Halsey National Forest

1422. What is the climate in Nebraska?
Humid continental in the east, and semi-arid climate

1423. What are the natural resources in Nebraska?
Soil and water

1424. What are the natural hazards in Nebraska?
Tornados, blizzards, and floods

1425. What are the major industries in Nebraska?
Farming (corn, soybeans, wheat, sorghum), grain processing, and meat-packing

Nevada

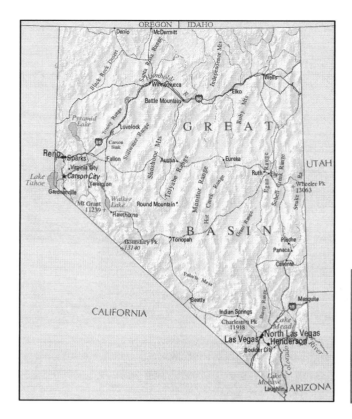

1426. Which states border Nevada in the north?
Oregon and Idaho

1427. Which state borders Nevada in the southeast?
Arizona

1428. Which state borders Nevada in the east?
Utah

1429. Which state borders Nevada in the west and southwest?
California

1430. Which river makes up the southeastern boundary of Nevada?
Colorado River

1431. What are the nicknames of Nevada?
Silver State; Sagebrush State; Battle Born State

1432. What is the state motto of Nevada?
All for Our Country

1433. What is the state song of Nevada?
Home Means Nevada

1434. What are the state trees of Nevada?
Single Leaf Pinon and Bristlecone Pine

1435. What is the state flower of Nevada?
Sagebrush

1436. What is the state grass of Nevada?
Indian Ricegrass

1437. What is the state bird of Nevada?
Mountain Bluebird

1438. What is the state animal of Nevada?
Desert Bighorn Sheep

1439. What is the state reptile of Nevada?
Desert Tortoise

1440. What is the state fish of Nevada?
Lahontan Cutthroat Trout

1441. What is the state fossil of Nevada?
Ichthyosaur

1442. What is the state rock of Nevada?
Sandstone

1443. What is the state metal of Nevada?
Silver

1444. What is the state precious gemstone of Nevada?
Virgin Valley Black Fire Opal

1445. What is the state semi-precious gemstone of Nevada?
Turquoise

1446. What is the state artifact of Nevada?
Tule Duck

1447. What are the state colors of Nevada?
Silver and Blue

1448. What is the capital of Nevada?
Carson City (the largest city by area)

1449. What is the largest city by population in Nevada?
Las Vegas

1450. Who claimed Nevada in 1519, although no exploration occurred?
Spain

1451. Who entered Nevada in 1776?
Francisco Garcés (Spanish missionary)

1452. Who took control of the Nevada area in 1821?
Mexico

1453. Who explored the Las Vegas Valley in 1827?
Jedediah Strong Smith (American explorer)

1454. Who traveled the Humboldt River in 1828?
Peter Skene Ogden (Canadian explorer)

1455. By which treaty was Nevada granted to the United States in 1848?
Treaty of Guadalupe Hidalgo

1456. When was the Territory of Nevada established, split from the Territory of Utah?
March 2nd, 1861

1457. When was Nevada admitted to the Union?
October 31st, 1864 (36th)

1458. What is the area of Nevada?
110,562 sq mi / 286,367 km^2 (7th)

1459. Approximately what percentage of Nevada is federally owned?

85%
1460. What is the population of Nevada?
2,839,099 (by 2014)
1461. What is the topography of Nevada?
Basin and Range Province; Great Basin in the north and south; Sierra Nevada Mountains in the west
1462. What is the highest point of Nevada, located in the White Mountains?
Boundary Peak (13,147 ft / 4,007 m)
1463. What is the lowest point of Nevada?
Colorado River at California border (481 ft / 147 m)
1464. What are the major rivers in Nevada?
Colorado River, Humboldt River, and Truckee River
1465. What are the major lakes in Nevada?
Pyramid Lake, Lake Mead, Lake Mojave, Lake Tahoe, and Walker Lake
1466. Which lake, located in the Sierra Nevada, is the 2nd deepest in United States?
Lake Tahoe (1,645 ft / 501 m)
1467. What is Lake Tahoe's rank by size in alpine lakes in North America?
1st (191 sq mi / 490 km^2)
1468. Hoover Dam in the Black Canyon of the Colorado River forms which lake?
Lake Mead
1469. Which national parks are located in Nevada?
Death Valley National Park (in California and Nevada, 5,262 sq mi / 13,629 km^2) and Great Basin National Park (121 sq mi / 312 km^2)
1470. What is Great Basin National Park famous for?
Groves of ancient bristlecone pines, the oldest known non-clonal organisms, and the Lehman Caves at the base of Wheeler Peak
1471. Who in 1895 invented the first slot machine, Liberty Bell, which became the model for all slots to follow?
Charles Fey (San Francisco)
1472. Nevada has about how many slot machines for every 100 residents?
10
1473. Which city in Nevada claims to be the Entertainment Capital of the World?
Las Vegas
1474. Which city in Nevada is known as the Biggest Little City in the World?
Reno
1475. What is the climate in Nevada?
Desert and semiarid
1476. What are the natural resources in Nevada?
Mineral deposits (copper, mercury, tungsten, gold, silver), wildlife, and beautiful scenery
1477. What are the natural hazards in Nevada?
Earthquakes, floods, and storms
1478. What are the major industries in Nevada?
Gambling, tourism, mining (gold, silver), and hydro-electric power

New Hampshire

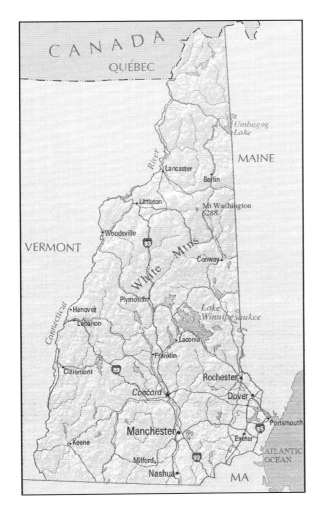

1479. Which state borders New Hampshire in the west?
   Vermont
1480. Which state borders New Hampshire in the south?
   Massachusetts
1481. Which state borders New Hampshire in the east?
   Maine
1482. Which country borders New Hampshire in the north?
   Canada
1483. Which river makes up the western boundary of New Hampshire?
   Connecticut River
1484. Which river makes up part of the eastern boundary of New Hampshire?
   Salmon Falls River
1485. Which water body lies to the east of New Hampshire?
   Atlantic Ocean
1486. What is the nickname of New Hampshire?
   Granite State

1487. What is the state motto of New Hampshire?
Live Free or Die

1488. What is the state song of New Hampshire?
Old New Hampshire

1489. What is the state tree of New Hampshire?
White Birch

1490. What is the state flower of New Hampshire?
Purple Lilac

1491. What is the state wildflower of New Hampshire?
Pink Lady's Slipper

1492. What is the state fruit of New Hampshire?
Pumpkin

1493. What is the state bird of New Hampshire?
Purple Finch

1494. What is the state animal of New Hampshire?
White-tailed Deer

1495. What is the state insect of New Hampshire?
Ladybug

1496. What is the state butterfly of New Hampshire?
Karner Blue Butterfly

1497. What is the state amphibian of New Hampshire?
Red-spotted Newt

1498. What is the state saltwater game of New Hampshire?
Striped Bass

1499. What is the state freshwater game of New Hampshire?
Brook Trout

1500. What is the state rock of New Hampshire?
Granite

1501. What is the state mineral of New Hampshire?
Beryl

1502. What is the state gem of New Hampshire?
Smoky Quartz

1503. What is the state sport of New Hampshire?
Skiing

1504. What is the state emblem of New Hampshire?
An elliptical panel with a picture of the Old Man of the Mountain surrounded on the top by the state name and on the bottom by the state motto, Live Free or Die

1505. When did the Old Man of the Mountain, the jagged profile of a face composed by a series of five granite cliff ledges on Cannon Mountain in the White Mountains, collapse?
May 3rd, 2003

1506. What is the capital of New Hampshire?
Concord (the largest city by area)

1507. What is the largest city by population in New Hampshire?
Manchester

1508. Who explored New Hampshire in 1603?

Martin Pring (English explorer)

1509. Which town is the first European settlement in New Hampshire, settled by William Berry in 1623?
Rye (near Portsmouth)

1510. Which city is the oldest permanent European settlement in New Hampshire, settled by brothers William and Edward Hilton in 1623?
Dover

1511. In which year did New Hampshire become part of Massachusetts rule?
1641

1512. In which year did New Hampshire separate from Massachusetts to be the Province of New Hampshire, a British colony?
1679

1513. When was New Hampshire admitted to the Union?
June 21st, 1788 (9th)

1514. What is the area of New Hampshire?
9,304 sq mi / 24,217 km^2 (46th)

1515. What is the population of New Hampshire?
1,326,813 (by 2014)

1516. What is the topography of New Hampshire?
Great North Woods in the north; White Mountains range in the northern center; Lake Regions (Lake Winnipesaukee, Winnisquam Lake, Squam Lake, and Newfound Lake) in the eastern center; Merrimack Valley and Connecticut River Valley in the south; Isles of Shoals (a group of small islands and tidal ledges) off the eastern coast

1517. What is the highest point of New Hampshire, located in the Presidential Range?
Mount Washington (6,288 ft / 1,917 m)

1518. What is the lowest point of New Hampshire?
Atlantic Ocean (0 ft / 0 m)

1519. How long is the coastline of New Hampshire?
18 mi / 29 km (23rd)

1520. What are the major rivers in New Hampshire?
Androscoggin River, Connecticut River, and Merrimack River

1521. What is the major lake in New Hampshire?
Lake Winnipesaukee

1522. In which town of New Hampshire was the first potato in the United States planted in 1719?
Derry (was part of Londonderry)

1523. Levi Hutchins, resident of which city in New Hampshire, invented the first alarm clock in 1787?
Concord

1524. In which town of New Hampshire was the first free public library in the United States founded on April 9th, 1833 by Abiel Abbot (Unitarian minister)?
Peterborough

1525. Which town is the smallest in New Hampshire (0.8 square mi / 2 km^2), composed of one large island and several smaller islands?
New Castle

1526. What is the climate in New Hampshire?

Humid continental

1527. What are the natural resources in New Hampshire?
    Soils, clays, loam, forests, and granites deposits

1528. What are the natural hazards in New Hampshire?
    Hurricanes and blizzards

1529. What are the major industries in New Hampshire?
    Textiles, lumber, tourism, electronic equipment, and software

New Jersey

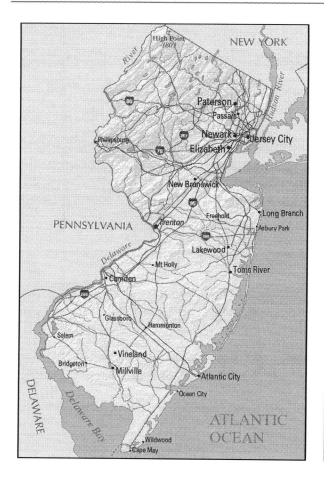

1530. Which state borders New Jersey in the north and northeast?
    New York

1531. Which state borders New Jersey in the west?
    Pennsylvania

1532. Which state lies to the southwest of New Jersey, across the Delaware Bay?
    Delaware

1533. Which river makes up the western boundary of New Jersey?
    Delaware River

1534. Which water bodies lie to the east of New Jersey?
Atlantic Ocean, Hudson River, Upper New York Bay, Kill Van Kull, Newark Bay, and Arthur Kill

1535. Which island is an exclave of New York in New Jersey waters?
Liberty Island (in Upper New York Bay)

1536. Which two islands in New Jersey has portions that belong to New York?
Ellis Island (Upper New York Bay) and Shooter's Island (in Newark Bay)

1537. What is the nickname of New Jersey?
Garden State; Diner Capital of the World

1538. What is the state motto of New Jersey?
Liberty and Prosperity

1539. What is the state tree of New Jersey?
Red Oak

1540. What is the state flower of New Jersey?
Purple Violet

1541. What is the state fruit of New Jersey?
Blueberry

1542. What is the state bird of New Jersey?
Eastern Goldfinch

1543. What is the state mammal of New Jersey?
Horse

1544. What is the state insect of New Jersey?
Honeybee

1545. What is the state shell of New Jersey?
Knobbed Whelk

1546. What is the state fish of New Jersey?
Brook Trout

1547. What is the state dinosaur of New Jersey?
Hadrosaurus Foulkii

1548. What is the state folk dance of New Jersey?
Square Dance

1549. What is the capital of New Jersey?
Trenton

1550. What is the largest city by population in New Jersey?
Newark

1551. What is the largest city by area in New Jersey?
Toms River

1552. Who explored New Jersey in 1524?
Giovanni da Verrazzano (Italian explorer in the service of the French)

1553. Who explored Hudson Valley, including New Jersey, in 1609?
Henry Hudson (English navigator and explorer)

1554. Where did Dutch establish the first trading post in New Jersey in 1618?
Bergen (township)

1555. Which Swedish colony, including New Jersey, was founded in 1638?
New Sweden

1556. In which year did the Province of New Jersey, a British colony, establish?
1664

1557. When was New Jersey admitted to the Union?
December 18th, 1787 (3rd)

1558. What is the area of New Jersey?
8,721 sq mi / 22,608 km^2 (47th)

1559. What is the population of New Jersey?
8,938,175 (by 2014, the state with the highest population density)

1560. What is special about the population of New Jersey?
Highest population density in the United States; highest percent urban population (90%) in the United States; only state where all counties are classified as metropolitan areas

1561. What is the topography of New Jersey?
Appalachian valley and ridge in the northwestern corner; highlands in the northwest; Newark basin piedmont in the southeast of the northern region; inner coastal plain in the center; outer coastal plain in the south

1562. What is the highest point of New Jersey, located in the Kittatinny Mountains?
High Point (1,803 ft / 550 m)

1563. What is the lowest point of New Jersey?
Atlantic (0 ft / 0 m)

1564. How long is the coastline of New Jersey?
130 mi / 209 km (13th)

1565. What are the major rivers in New Jersey?
Delaware River and Hudson River

1566. What is the largest lake in New Jersey?
Lake Hopatcong (4 sq mi / 10 km²)

1567. Which city in New Jersey is the Car Theft Capital of the World?
North Jersey

1568. Which city in New Jersey has the longest boardwalk in the world?
Atlantic City

1569. The first recorded baseball game in the United States was played in which city of New Jersey in 1846?
Hoboken

1570. The first intercollegiate football game in the United States was played in which city of New Jersey in 1869?
New Brunswick

1571. Which city in New Jersey is home to the Miss America pageant since 1921?
Atlantic City

1572. The first drive-in movie theatre in the world was opened in which city of New Jersey on June 6th, 1933?
Camden

1573. Casinos and legalized gambling were opened in which city of New Jersey in 1978?
Atlantic City

1574. Which township in New Jersey was named in honor of inventor Thomas Edison, who invented the light bulb, phonograph (record player), and motion picture projector in his Menlo Park laboratory?

Edison
1575. The largest seaport in the United States is located in which city of New Jersey?
Elizabeth
1576. What is special about the highways and railroads system in New Jersey?
The densest system in the United States
1577. Which suspension bridge, between New Jersey and New York on the Hudson River, was first opened on October 24th, 1931?
George Washington Bridge
1578. What is the climate of New Jersey?
Mostly humid mesothermal; humid continental in the northwest
1579. What are the natural resources in New Jersey?
Fertile soils and small deposits of minerals
1580. What are the natural hazards in New Jersey?
Hurricanes, tornados, winter storms, and floods
1581. What are the major industries in New Jersey?
Farming (potatoes, tomatoes, peaches), chemicals, pharmaceuticals, petroleum-based products, insurance, and tourism

New Mexico

1582. Which state borders New Mexico in the north?
Colorado
1583. Which state borders New Mexico in the east and south?
Texas
1584. Which state borders New Mexico in the east?
Oklahoma
1585. Which state touches New Mexico in the northwest?
Utah
1586. Which state borders New Mexico in the west?
Arizona
1587. Which country borders New Mexico in the south?
Mexico
1588. Which river runs the entire length of New Mexico?
Rio Grande
1589. What is the nickname of New Mexico?
Land of Enchantment
1590. What is the state motto of New Mexico?
It Grows as It Goes
1591. What is the state song of New Mexico?
O, Fair New Mexico
1592. What is the state tree of New Mexico?
Pinon
1593. What is the state flower of New Mexico?
Yucca

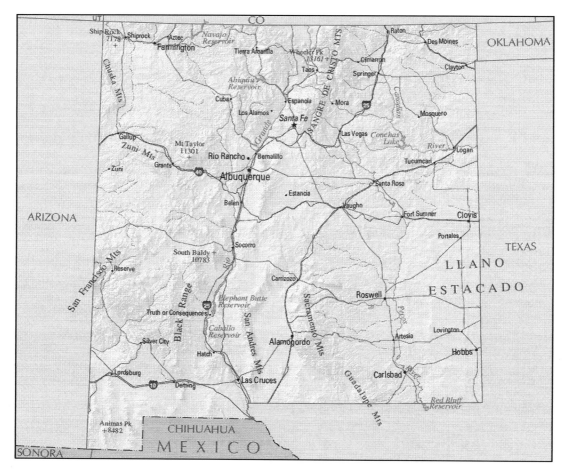

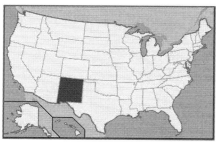

1594. What is the state grass of New Mexico?
Blue Gramma Grass
1595. What are the state vegetables of New Mexico?
Chile and Frijoles
1596. What is the state bird of New Mexico?
Roadrunner
1597. What is the state mammal of New Mexico?
Black Bear
1598. What is the state fish of New Mexico?

New Mexico Cutthroat Trout

1599. What is the state insect of New Mexico?
Tarantula Hawk Wasp

1600. What is the state dinosaur of New Mexico?
Coelophysis

1601. What is the state gem of New Mexico?
Turquoise

1602. What are the state colors of New Mexico?
Red and Yellow

1603. What is the state cookie of New Mexico?
Bizcochito

1604. What is the capital of New Mexico?
Santa Fe

1605. What is the largest city by population and area in New Mexico?
Albuquerque

1606. Who began rumors of the Seven Cities of Cibola Gold in 1536?
Cabeza de Vaca (Spanish explorer)

1607. Who discovered the Grand Canyon while searching for gold in 1540?
Francisco Vásquez de Coronado (Spanish conquistador)

1608. Which explorer founded the first European (Spanish) settlement, San Juan de los Caballeros, in New Mexico on July 11th, 1598?
Juan de Oñate (Spanish explorer)

1609. Northeastern New Mexico was purchased from France by which treaty signed on April 30th, 1803?
Louisiana Purchase

1610. What was the Santa Fe Trail that opened in 1822?
A 19th century transportation route through central North America that connected Missouri with Santa Fe

1611. What was the Old Spanish Trail?
A historical trade route which connected the northern New Mexico settlements near Santa Fe with that of California in 1829

1612. By which treaty was most of New Mexico granted to the United States in 1848?
Treaty of Guadalupe Hidalgo

1613. When was the Territory of New Mexico established?
September 9th, 1850

1614. When did the Gadsden Purchase acquire the southwestern New Mexico for the United States?
December 30th, 1853

1615. When was New Mexico admitted to the Union?
January 6th, 1912 (47th)

1616. What is the area of New Mexico?
121,589 sq mi / 315,194 km^2 (5th)

1617. What is the population of New Mexico?
2,085,572 (by 2014)

1618. What is the topography of New Mexico?

Mostly covered by mountains, high plains, and desert; Great Plains in the east; Sangre de Cristo Mountains (the southernmost part of the Rocky Mountains) in the north; San Juan Basin in the northwest; basin and range in the southwest; Chihuahuan Desert in the south

1619. What is the highest point of New Mexico, located in the Taos Mountains?
Wheeler Peak (13,167 ft / 4,013 m)

1620. What is the lowest point of New Mexico?
Red Bluff Reservoir on Texas border (2,844 ft / 867 m)

1621. What are the major rivers in New Mexico?
Rio Grande and Pecos River

1622. What are the major lakes in New Mexico?
Elephant Butte Reservoir, Conchas Lake, and Navajo Reservoir

1623. With the lowest water-to-land ratio state in the United States, lakes and rivers make up what percentage of New Mexico total surface area?
0.002%

1624. Which national park is located in New Mexico?
Carlsbad Caverns National Park (73 sq mi / 189 km^2)

1625. What is Carlsbad Caverns National Park famous for?
117 caves (the longest one is 130 mi / 209 km long, and the biggest room is almost 4,000 ft / 1,220 m long, 625 ft / 191 m wide, and 255 ft /78 m high at the highest point)

1626. What is Santa Fe's rank by elevation among state capitals in the United States?
1st (7,199 feet / 2,134 m)

1627. Which city in New Mexico is known as the City of the Crosses?
Las Cruces

1628. Which city in New Mexico hosts the world's largest international hot air balloon fiesta every October since 1972?
Albuquerque

1629. Which city in New Mexico hosts the Whole Enchilada Fiesta, making the world's largest enchilada, every September since 1980?
Las Cruces

1630. Which city in New Mexico has been known as the Uranium Capital of the World?
Grants

1631. Which city in New Mexico hosts the Great American Duck Race, held on the 3rd weekend of August?
Deming

1632. The world's first Atomic Bomb was detonated on July 16th, 1945 on the White Sands Testing Range near which city in New Mexico?
Alamogordo

1633. Which town in New Mexico is known as the Green Chile Capital of the World?
Hatch

1634. What is the climate in New Mexico?
Generally semi-arid to arid, though there are areas of continental and alpine climates

1635. What are the natural resources in New Mexico?
Large mineral deposits and its renewable land-based resources (forests, grasses, plants, animals)

1636. What are the natural hazards in New Mexico?

Hurricanes and wildfires

1637. What are the major industries in New Mexico?
    Mining (potash, copper, silver, uranium), oil, natural gas, and tourism

New York

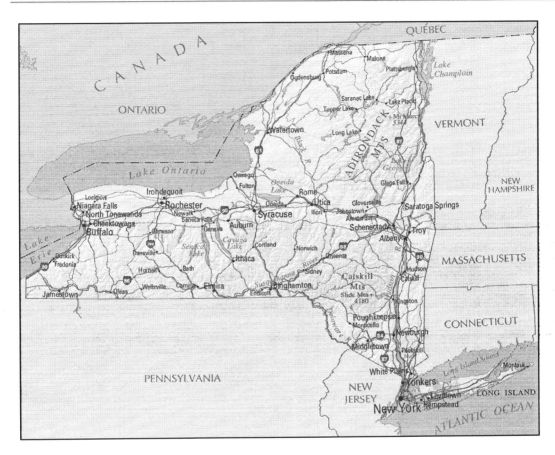

1638. Which states border New York in the east?
    Connecticut, Vermont, and Massachusetts

1639. Which states border New York in the south?
    New Jersey and Pennsylvania

1640. Which state lies to the northeast of Long Island, across the Long Island Sound?

Rhode Island

1641. Which country borders New York in the north and west?
Canada

1642. Which water body lies to the southeast of New York?
Atlantic Ocean

1643. Which water body is between New York and Vermont?
Lake Champlain

1644. Which water bodies are between New York and Canada?
Lake Erie and Lake Ontario

1645. What is the nickname of New York?
Empire State

1646. What is the state motto of New York?
Ever Upwards

1647. What is the state song of New York?
I Love New York

1648. What is the state tree of New York?
Sugar Maple

1649. What is the state flower of New York?
Rose

1650. What is the state fruit of New York?
Apple

1651. What is the state bird of New York?
Eastern Bluebird

1652. What is the state mammal of New York?
Beaver

1653. What is the state insect of New York?
Nine-spotted Ladybug

1654. What is the state fish of New York?
Brook Trout

1655. What is the state shell of New York?
Bay Scallop

1656. What is the state fossil of New York?
Sea Scorpion

1657. What is the state gem of New York?
Garnet

1658. What is the capital of New York?
Albany

1659. What is the largest city by population and area in New York?
New York City

1660. Who sailed into New York harbor in 1524?
Giovanni da Verrazzano (Italian explorer in the service of French)

1661. Who explored Hudson Valley, including New York in 1609?
Henry Hudson (English navigator and explorer)

1662. Who claimed the Lake Champlain area, including northeastern New York, for France in 1609?

Samuel de Champlain (French explorer)

1663. What was the oldest Dutch settlement in North America, founded in 1614 in New York?
Fort Nassau (the present-day Albany, the 3rd oldest continuously inhabited city in the United States)

1664. In which year did English conquer New Netherland and rename the colony and city to New York?
1664

1665. When was New York admitted to the Union?
July 26th, 1788 (11th)

1666. Which city in New York was the nation's capital during 1785 – 1790?
New York City

1667. When was George Washington inaugurated as the first United States' president in New York City?
April 16th, 1789

1668. What is the area of New York?
54,556 sq mi / 141,300 km^2 (27th)

1669. What is the population of New York?
19,746,227 (by 2014)

1670. What is the topography of New York?
Adirondack Mountains in the center; Allegheny Plateau in the south; Catskill Mountains in the southeast; Long Island in the extreme southeast

1671. What is the highest point of New York, located in the Adirondack Mountains?
Mount Marcy (5,343 ft / 1629 m)

1672. What is the lowest point of New York?
Atlantic Ocean (0 ft / 0 m)

1673. How long is the coastline of New York?
127 mi / 204 km (14th)

1674. What are the major rivers in New York?
Hudson River, Mohawk River, and Genesee River

1675. What are the major lakes in New York?
Lake Erie, Lake Ontario, Lake Champlain, and the Finger Lakes

1676. Which river begins at Lake Tear of the Clouds in New York and drains in Upper New York Bay in New York and New Jersey?
Hudson River

1677. Which canal in New York runs about 363 mi (584 km) from Albany on the Hudson River to Buffalo at Lake Erie, completing a navigable water route from the Atlantic Ocean to the Great Lakes?
Erie Canal

1678. What was the importance of the Erie Canal?
It turned New York City into a major port

1679. What is the nickname of Lake George, a long, narrow oligotrophic lake draining northwards into Lake Champlain and the St. Lawrence River Drainage basin?
Queen of American Lakes

1680. What are the Finger Lakes in Upstate New York?
A serious of lakes that are long and thin (resembling fingers), each oriented roughly on a

north-south axis

1681. What is the longest Finger Lake?
Cayuga (38 mi / 61 km)

1682. What is the largest Finger Lake by surface area?
Seneca Lake (67 sq mi / 173 km^2)

1683. Which Finger Lake is the deepest lake entirely within New York?
Seneca Lake (618 ft / 188 m)

1684. What is the largest lake by surface area entirely within New York, and it is sometimes referred to as the thumb of the Finger Lakes?
Oneida Lake (80 sq mi / 207 km^2)

1685. Which state park in New York is the largest park and the largest state-level protected area in the 48 contiguous United States, and the largest National Historic Landmark?
Adirondack Park (9,375 sq mi / 24,281 km^2)

1686. Which state park in New York was the first state park in the United States?
Niagara Falls State Park (originally called Niagara Reservation in 1885)

1687. In which city of New York was Washington's Headquarters State Historic Site, the first publicly owned historic site, built in 1750?
Newburgh

1688. What are nicknames of New York City?
Big Apple; Gotham; Center of the Universe; City That Never Sleeps; Capital of the World

1689. New York City consists of which five boroughs?
Bronx, Brooklyn, Manhattan, Queens, and Staten Island

1690. Besides Marble Hill on the mainland, Manhattan is located on which islands?
Manhattan Island, Roosevelt Island, Randall's Island, Wards Island, Governors Island, Liberty Island, part of Ellis Island, Mill Rock, and U Thant Island

1691. Which two boroughs of New York City are located on Long Island?
Brooklyn and Queens

1692. What is Downstate New York?
New York City, Long Island, and nearby areas

1693. What is Upstate New York?
North of the core of the New York metropolitan area in New York

1694. What was founded on May 17th, 1792 when the Buttonwood Agreement was signed by 24 stock brokers outside of 68 Wall Street?
New York Stock Exchange

1695. The United States Military Academy was established in 1802 at West Point of which town in New York?
Highlands

1696. Which bridge in New York connects Manhattan and Brooklyn, and it was the first steel-wire suspension bridge and the world's longest suspension bridge (1,595 ft / 486 m) during 1883 – 1903?
Brooklyn Bridge

1697. What is the colossal neoclassical sculpture on Liberty Island in New York Harbor, designed by Frédéric Bartholdi and dedicated on October 28th, 1886?
Statue of Liberty

1698. Which island in New York Harbor was the gateway for millions of immigrants to the United

State during 1892 – 1954?

Ellis Island

1699. The Great Depression, the longest, most widespread, and deepest worldwide economic depression of the 20th century, started with the New York Stock Exchange crash on which day known as Black Tuesday?

October 29th, 1929

1700. An Army Air Corps B-25 crashed into which building in New York City on July 28th, 1945?

Empire State Building

1701. The United Nations is headquartered in which city of New York since October 9th, 1952?

New York City

1702. Which highway system in New York was the longest toll road in the world when it was opened on June 24th, 1954?

Governor Thomas E. Dewey Thruway (9,570 mi / 917 km)

1703. Ellis Island was made part of the Statue of Liberty National Monument in which year?

1965

1704. A 1998 United States Supreme Court decision ruled most of the Ellis Island to be part of which state?

New Jersey

1705. In which city did the terrorists hijack and crash two planes into the World Trade Center on September 11th, 2011, with nearly 3,000 killed and billions in property loss?

New York City

1706. The Niagara Falls, the world's highest flow rate waterfall (64,750 cu ft/s or 1,834 m^3/s), is located 17 mi (27 km) from which city in New York?

Buffalo

1707. Which city in New York is the home of the world's smallest church (3.5 in X 6 in / 1.1 m X 1.8 m)?

Oneida

1708. Which city in New York is nicknamed as Flour City, Flower City, and World's Image Centre?

Rochester

1709. In which city of New York did Gennaro Lombardi open Lombardi's in 1905, the first pizzeria in the United States?

New York City

1710. What is the climate in New York?

Humid continental

1711. What are the natural resources in New York?

Fertile soil, mineral varieties, and abundant water supplies

1712. What are the natural hazards in New York?

Hurricanes, tornados, and winter storms

1713. What are the major industries in New York?

Finance, communications, international trade, publishing, fashion, communications, farming (fruit and dairy), and tourism

North Carolina

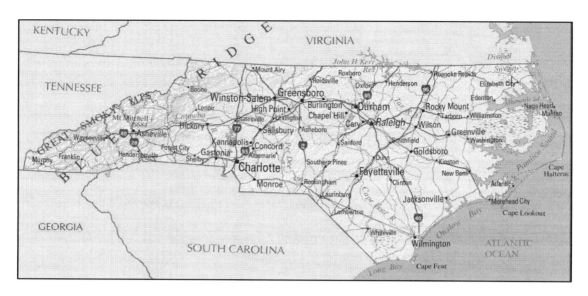

1714. Which state borders North Carolina in the north?
   Virginia

1715. Which state borders South Carolina in the south?
   South Carolina and Georgia

1716. Which state borders North Carolina in the west?
   Tennessee

1717. Which water body lies to the east of North Carolina?
   Atlantic Ocean

1718. What are the nicknames of North Carolina?
   Tar Heel State; Old North State

1719. What is the state motto of North Carolina?
   To Be Rather Than to Seem

1720. What is the state song of North Carolina?
   The Old North State

1721. What is the state tree of North Carolina?
   Longleaf Pine

1722. What is the state flower of North Carolina?
   Flowering Dogwood

1723. What is the state vegetable of North Carolina?
   Sweet Potato

1724. What is the state bird of North Carolina?
Cardinal
1725. What is the state mammal of North Carolina?
Gray Squirrel
1726. What is the state dog of North Carolina?
Plott Hound
1727. What is the state shell of North Carolina?
Scotch Bonnet
1728. What is the state reptile of North Carolina?
Eastern Box Turtle
1729. What is the state fish of North Carolina?
Channel Bass
1730. What is the state rock of North Carolina?
Granite
1731. What is the state precious stone of North Carolina?
Emerald
1732. What is the state soil of North Carolina?
North Carolina Cecil
1733. What are the state colors of North Carolina?
Red and Blue
1734. What is the state beverage of North Carolina?
Milk
1735. What is the state historic boat of North Carolina?
Shad Boat
1736. What is the capital of North Carolina?
Raleigh
1737. What is the largest city by population and area in North Carolina?
Charlotte
1738. Who explored North Carolina in 1540?
Hernando de Soto (Spanish explorer)
1739. Who established the first English colony in North America on Roanoke Island in 1585?
Sir Walter Raleigh (English explorer)
1740. Why was the Roanoke Colony called Lost Colony?
Because the colony mysteriously vanished with no trace except for the word "Croatoan" scrawled on a nearby tree
1741. What was the oldest town in North Carolina, incorporated in 1705?
Bath
1742. In which year was the Province of North Carolina, a British colony, established?
1729
1743. When was North Carolina admitted to the Union?
November 21st, 1789 (12th)
1744. During which period did North Carolina secede from the Union?
1861 – 1868
1745. What is the area of North Carolina?
53,819 sq mi / 139,581 km^2 (28th)

1746. What is the population of North Carolina?
9,943,964 (by 2014)
1747. What is the topography of North Carolina?
Appalachian Mountains (Blue Ridge Mountains and Great Smoky Mountains) in the west;
Piedmont Plateau in the center; Coastal Plain in the east; Outer Banks in the extreme east
1748. What is the highest point of North Carolina, located in the Appalachian Mountains?
Mount Mitchell (6,684 ft / 2,037 m, the highest peak of the Appalachian Mountains)
1749. What is the lowest point of North Carolina?
Atlantic Ocean (0 ft / 0 m)
1750. How long is the coastline of North Carolina?
301 mi / 484 km (7th)
1751. What are the major rivers in North Carolina?
Neuse River, Roanoke River, and Yadkin River
1752. What are the major lakes in North Carolina?
Lake Mattamuskeet, Lake Phelps, and Lake Waccamaw
1753. Which national park is located in North Carolina?
Great Smoky Mountains National Park (in North Carolina and Tennessee, 814 sq mi / 2,110 km^2)
1754. What is the Great Smoky Mountains National Park famous for?
A wide range of elevation with over 400 vertebrate species, 100 tree species, and 5000 plant species, as well as over 800 miles (1,300 km) of hiking trails
1755. Grandfather Mountain, the highest peak in the Blue Ridge, was the only private park in the world designated by the United Nations as an International Biosphere Reserve until it was purchased by whom on September 29th, 2008 for $12 million?
North Carolina State government
1756. Grandfather Mountain is famous for its mile-high swinging bridge, the highest in the United State that was built in which year?
1952
1757. Which university in North Caroline was the first public university in the United States to admit students, although it was not the first chartered public university?
University of North Carolina Chapel Hill (1795)
1758. The Wright Brothers made the first successful powered flight by man in which town of North Carolina on the Outer Banks on December 17th, 1903?
Kill Devil Hill
1759. Which city in North Carolina is known as the Furniture Capital of the World?
High Point
1760. Which city in North Carolina is home to the North Carolina Seafood Festival, held the first weekend in October, since May 5th, 2007?
Morehead City
1761. Which city in North Carolina is home to Biltmore House, the largest privately-owned home in the United States (135,000 sq ft /12,500 m^2 and featuring 250 rooms)?
Asheville
1762. Which dam on the Little Tennessee River is the tallest dam in the Eastern United States?
Fontana Dam (480 ft / 150 m)
1763. What are the nicknames of Fayetteville in North Carolina?

All-American City; Old Capitol; Fayette City; Military-Town; Campbellton; Fayettenam; Southeast Paris; Mini-Golf Town; Apartment City; Brokeville, USA; Shermville

1764. Which town in North Carolina was known as the Fish Town in the early 1700's?
Beaufort

1765. The Research Triangle Park (RTP) is the prominent high-tech research and development centers in the triangle region defined by which three cities in North Carolina?
Durham, Raleigh, and Chapel Hill

1766. What is the climate in North Carolina?
Mostly humid subtropical; subtropical highland in the higher elevations of the Appalachian Mountains

1767. What are the natural resources in North Carolina?
Rich soils, mineral deposits, and thick forests

1768. What are the natural hazards in North Carolina?
Hurricanes, tornados, and winter storms

1769. What are the major industries in North Carolina?
Farming (tobacco, poultry), textiles, and furniture

North Dakota

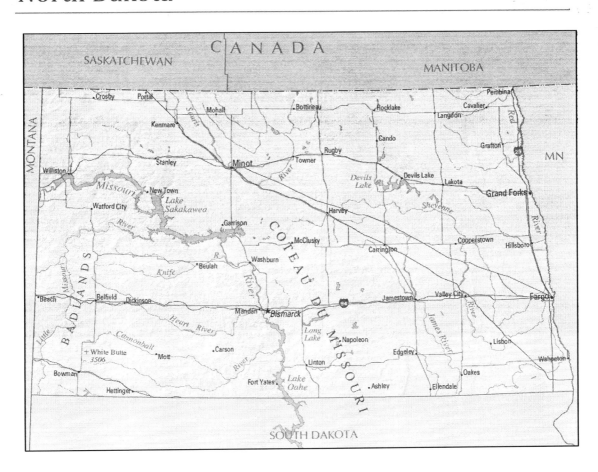

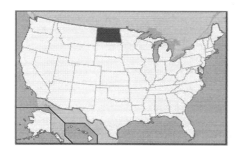

1770. Which state borders North Dakota in the east?
Minnesota
1771. Which state borders North Dakota in the south?
South Dakota
1772. Which state borders North Dakota in the west?
Montana
1773. Which country borders North Dakota in the north?
Canada
1774. Which river makes up the eastern boundary of North Dakota?
Red River
1775. What are the nicknames of North Dakota?
Peace Garden State; Roughrider State; Flickertail State; Norse Dakota; The 701; Heaven
1776. What is the state motto of North Dakota?
Liberty and Union, Now and Forever, One and Inseparable
1777. What is the state song of North Dakota?
North Dakota
1778. What is the state tree of North Dakota?
American Elm
1779. What is the state flower of North Dakota?
Wild Prairie Rose
1780. What is the state grass of North Dakota?
Western Wheatgrass
1781. What is the state bird of North Dakota?
Western Meadowlark
1782. What is the state fish of North Dakota?
Northern Pike
1783. What is the state honorary equine of North Dakota?
Nokota Breed
1784. What is the state fossil of North Dakota?
Teredo Petrified Wood
1785. What is the state beverage of North Dakota?
Milk
1786. What is the state dance of North Dakota?
Square Dance
1787. What is the capital of North Dakota?
Bismarck

1788. What is the largest city by population and area in North Dakota?
Fargo
1789. Who claimed Hudson Bay watershed for England, including eastern North Dakota, in 1610?
Henry Hudson (English navigator and explorer)
1790. Who navigated the Mississippi River and claimed for France all lands drained by the river and its tributaries, including North Dakota, in 1682?
Robert de LaSalle (French explorer)
1791. Who was the first European to explore North Dakota at the Mandan tribes in 1738?
Pierre Gaultier de Varennes (French Canadian military officer, fur trader, and explorer)
1792. Which city in North Dakota was the first European settlement in the Dakotas, founded in 1797?
Pembina
1793. Most of North Dakota was purchased from France by which treaty signed on April 30th, 1803?
Louisiana Purchase
1794. When was the Territory of Dakota established, splitting from the Territory of Nebraska?
March 2nd, 1861
1795. When was North Dakota admitted to the Union?
November 2nd, 1889 (39th)
1796. What is the area of North Dakota?
70,700 sq mi / 183,272 km^2 (19th)
1797. What is the population of North Dakota?
739,482 (by 2014)
1798. What is the topography of North Dakota?
Hilly Great Plains in the western half; Drift Prairie and Missouri Plateau in the center; Red River Valley in the east; Badlands in the southwest
1799. What is the highest point of North Dakota, located in the Badlands?
White Butte (3,508 ft / 1,069 m)
1800. What is the lowest point of North Dakota?
Red River of the North at Canada border
1801. What are the major rivers in North Dakota?
James River, Missouri River, and Red River
1802. What are the major lakes in North Dakota?
Lake Sakakawea and Lake Ohe
1803. Which national park is located in North Dakota?
Theodore Roosevelt National Park (110 sq mi / 285 km^2)
1804. What is the Theodore Roosevelt National Park famous for?
3 geographically separated areas of badlands
1805. Which park is located on the international border between North Dakota and Canada?
International Peace Garden
1806. Which city in North Dakota claims to be the geographic center of North America, with a monument featuring flags of the United States, Canada, and Mexico?
Rugby
1807. Which city in North Dakota is located in a large, flat, and ancient dried lake bottom surrounded by some of the most fertile farmland in the world?

Hillsboro

1808. Which city in North Dakota was named after the slogan "Hope of the West"?
Westhope

1809. Which city in North Dakota claims to be the Goose Capital of North Dakota?
Kenmare

1810. Which city in North Dakota claims to be the Perch Capital of the World?
Devils Lake

1811. What is the nickname of Bottineau in North Dakota?
Four Seasons Playground

1812. What is the nickname of Jamestown in North Dakota?
Buffalo City

1813. What is the climate in North Dakota?
Semi-arid

1814. What are the natural resources in North Dakota?
Fertile soil and large mineral deposits including petroleum, coal, natural gas and sand and gravel

1815. What are the natural hazards in North Dakota?
Tornados, blizzard, and floods

1816. What are the major industries in North Dakota?
Farming (wheat, barley, oats, flaxseed), cattle, mining (lignite, soft coal), and electrical power generation

Ohio

1817. Which state borders Ohio in the north?
Michigan

1818. Which state borders Ohio in the west?
Indiana

1819. Which state borders Ohio in the southeast?
West Virginia

1820. Which state borders Ohio in the south?
Kentucky

1821. Which state borders Ohio in the east?
Pennsylvania

1822. Which river makes up the southern and southeast boundaries of Ohio?
Ohio River

1823. Which water body lies to the north of Ohio?
Lake Erie

1824. Which country lies to the north of Ohio, across Lake Erie?
Canada

1825. What are the nicknames of Ohio?
Buckeye State; Mother of Presidents; Birthplace of Aviation; Heart of It All

1826. What is the state motto of Ohio?
With God, All Things Are Possible

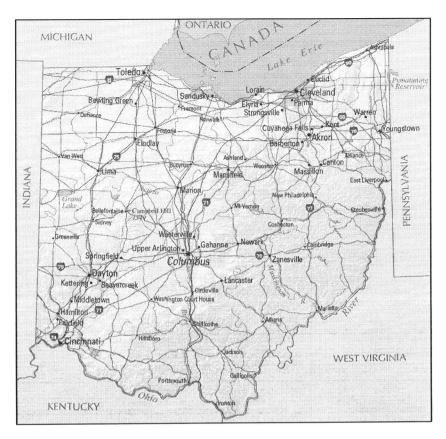

1827. What is the state song of Ohio?
Beautiful Ohio

1828. What is the official state rock song of Ohio?
Hang On Sloopy

1829. What is the state tree of Ohio?
Buckeye

1830. What is the state flower of Ohio?
Scarlet Carnation

1831. What is the state bird of Ohio?
Cardinal

1832. What is the state mammal of Ohio?

White-tailed Deer

1833. What is the state insect of Ohio?
Ladybug

1834. What is the state reptile of Ohio?
Black Racer Snake

1835. What is the state beverage of Ohio?
Tomato Juice

1836. What is the state fossil of Ohio?
Trilobite Isotelus

1837. What is the state gemstone of Ohio?
Flint

1838. What is the capital of Ohio?
Columbus (the largest city by population and area)

1839. Who surveyed the Ohio area and claimed the entire region for France in 1669?
Robert de LaSalle (French explorer)

1840. In which year did the Britain control Ohio after the decisive victory of the French and Indian War?
1763

1841. When was the Territory Northwest of the River Ohio established?
July 13th, 1787

1842. Which city was the first permanent European settlement in the Territory Northwest of the River Ohio, founded by Rufus Putnam (French general) in 1788?
Marietta

1843. When was Ohio admitted to the Union?
March 1st, 1803 (17th)

1844. What is the area of Ohio?
44,825 sq mi / 116,096 km^2 (34th)

1845. What is the population of Ohio?
11,594,163 (by 2014)

1846. What is the topography of Ohio?
Great Black Swamp in the northwest; flat in the central area and in the east

1847. What is the highest point of Ohio?
Campbell Hill (1,549 ft / 472 m)

1848. What is the lowest point of Ohio?
Ohio River (455 ft / 139 m)

1849. What are the major rivers in Ohio?
Arkansas River, Canadian River, and Red River

1850. What are the major lakes in Ohio?
Lake Texoma, Eufaula Lake, Lake Hudson, Lake O' the Cherokees, Gibson Lake, Oologah Lake, and Keystone Lake

1851. Which national park is located in Ohio?
Cuyahoga Valley National Park (51 sq mi / 133 km^2)

1852. What is the Cuyahoga Valley National Park famous for?
Waterfalls, hills, trails, and displays about early rural living

1853. The first traffic light in the United States started at which city in Ohio on Aug 5th, 1914?

Cleveland

1854. Which city in Ohio became the world's first city to be lighted electrically in 1879?
Cleveland

1855. What are the nicknames of Cleveland?
Forest City; Metropolis of the Western Reserve; Sixth City; Rock 'n' Roll Capital of the World; C-Town; North Coast

1856. What are the nicknames of Akron?
Rubber City; City of Invention

1857. The Ohio and Erie Canal, opened in 1832, connected which two cities in Ohio?
Akron and Cleveland

1858. Which city in Ohio is situated in three counties (Seneca, Hancock & Wood)?
Fostoria

1859. What is the nickname of the village of Dresden?
Basket Village USA

1860. What is the climate in Ohio?
Humid continental

1861. What are the natural resources in Ohio?
Fertile soils and valuable mineral deposits such as coal, oil, natural gas, and rock salt

1862. What are the natural hazards in Ohio?
Tornados, winter storms, floods, and earthquakes

1863. What are the major industries in Ohio?
Manufacturing (steel, cars, airplanes, rubber products, chemicals, plastics), farming, and mining (coal)

Oklahoma

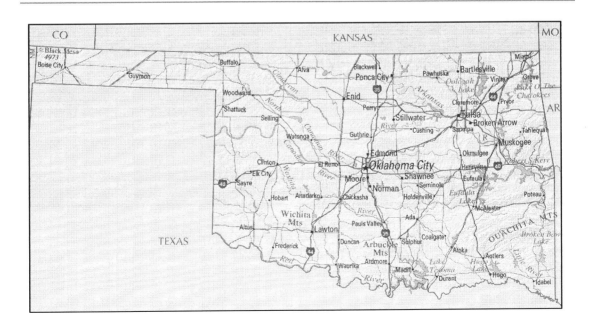

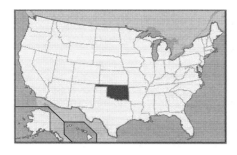

1864. Which states border Oklahoma in the north?
Colorado and Kansas

1865. Which states border Oklahoma in the east?
Arkansas and Missouri

1866. Which state borders Oklahoma in the south and southwest?
Texas

1867. Which state borders Oklahoma in the west?
New Mexico

1868. Which rivers make up the southern boundary of Oklahoma?
Red River

1869. What is the nickname of Oklahoma?
Sooner State

1870. What is the state motto of Oklahoma?
Hard Work Conquers All

1871. What is the state song of Oklahoma?
Oklahoma!

1872. What is the state tree of Oklahoma?
Redbud

1873. What is the state flower of Oklahoma?
Oklahoma Rose

1874. What is the state wildflower of Oklahoma?
Indian Blanket

1875. What is the state floral emblem of Oklahoma?
Mistletoe

1876. What is the state grass of Oklahoma?
Indiangrass

1877. What is the state bird of Oklahoma?
Yellowhammer

1878. What is the state bird of Oklahoma?
Scissor-tailed Flycatcher

1879. What is the state game bird of Oklahoma?
Wild Turkey

1880. What is the state animal of Oklahoma?
Buffalo

1881. What is the state game mammal of Oklahoma?
White-tailed Deer

1882. What is the state furbearer of Oklahoma?

Raccoon

1883. What is the state insect of Oklahoma?

Honeybee

1884. What is the state butterfly of Oklahoma?

Black Swallowtail

1885. What is the state reptile of Oklahoma?

Collared Lizard

1886. What is the state fish of Oklahoma?

White Bass (also called Sand Bass)

1887. What is the state dinosaur of Oklahoma?

Acrocanthosaurus Atokensis

1888. What is the state fossil of Oklahoma?

Saurophaganax Maximus

1889. What is the state rock of Oklahoma?

Rose Rock

1890. What is the state soil of Oklahoma?

Port Silt Loam

1891. What is the state beverage of Oklahoma?

Milk

1892. What is the state percussive musical instrument of Oklahoma?

Drum

1893. What is the state waltz of Oklahoma?

Oklahoma Wind

1894. What are the state colors of Oklahoma?

Green and White

1895. What is the state dance of Oklahoma?

Square Dance

1896. What is the capital of Oklahoma?

Oklahoma City (the largest city by population and area)

1897. Who claimed Oklahoma for France in 1682?

Robert de LaSalle (French explorer)

1898. Oklahoma was purchased from France by which treaty signed on April 30th, 1803?

Louisiana Purchase

1899. Which five Native American tribes, called the Five Civilized Tribes, were forced to relocate from their native lands by the United States government into Oklahoma, known then as the Indian Territory, during 1830s – 1840s?

Cherokee, Chickasaw, Choctaw, Creek and Seminole

1900. How many additional Native American tribes were moved to Oklahoma during 1870s?

25

1901. What was the Land Run of 1889?

The United States government opened all unassigned Oklahoma lands for settlement, and thousands of settlers crossed the border to stake their claims

1902. The settlers that entered to claim land before the official start of the land run are called what?

Sooners

1903. When was the Territory of Oklahoma established, coexisted with the Indian Territory?
May 2nd, 1890

1904. When was Oklahoma admitted to the Union, both the Territory of Oklahoma and the Indian Territory?
November 16th, 1907 (46th)

1905. What is the area of Oklahoma?
69,898 sq mi / 181,195 km^2 (20th)

1906. What is the population of Oklahoma?
3,878,051 (by 2014)

1907. What is the topography of Oklahoma?
Nearly flat in the west with some hills in the central and eastern region; slopes downwards towards the east

1908. What is the highest point of Oklahoma?
Black Mesa (4,975 ft / 1516 m)

1909. What is the lowest point of Oklahoma?
Little River (289 ft / 88 m)

1910. What are the major rivers in Oklahoma?
Tombigbee River, Oklahoma River, Tennessee River, and Chattahoochee River

1911. What are the major lakes in Oklahoma?
Guntersville Lake, Wilson Lake, West Point Lake, and Lewis Smith Lake

1912. The world's first installed parking meter was in which city of Oklahoma on July 16th, 1935?
Oklahoma City

1913. The McClellan-Kerr Arkansas River Navigation System (MKARNS), opened June 5th, 1971, is part of the inland waterway system originating at the Tulsa Port of which city and running southeast through Oklahoma and Arkansas to the Mississippi River?
Catoosa

1914. What is the oldest chartered town in Oklahoma?
Choctaw (1893)

1915. The terrorists bombed the Alfred P. Murrah Federal Building in which city of Oklahoma on April 19th, 1995?
Oklahoma City

1916. Which city in Oklahoma claims to be the Indian Capital of the Nation?
Anadarko

1917. Which city in Oklahoma claims to be the Deer Capital of the World and the Gateway to Southeast Oklahoma?
Antlers

1918. What is the climate in Oklahoma?
Long and hot summers; mild winters

1919. What are the natural resources in Oklahoma?
Fertile soil, abundant water, fine growing climate, and vast mineral reserves of petroleum (among the largest in the country) and natural gas

1920. What are the natural hazards in Oklahoma?
Hurricanes, tornados, winter storms, and wildfires

1921. What are the major industries in Oklahoma?

Farming (wheat, cattle), oil, and natural gas

Oregon

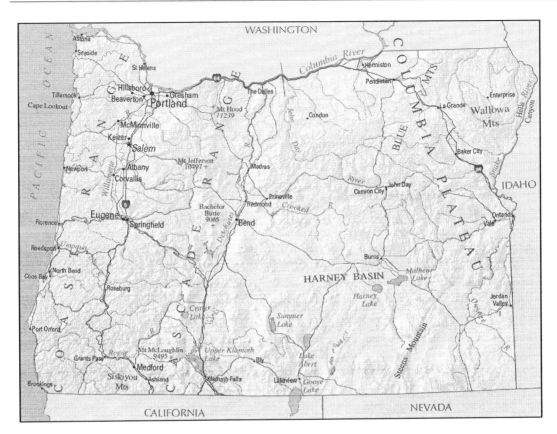

1922. Which state borders Oregon in the north?
Washington

1923. Which state borders Oregon in the east?
Idaho

1924. Which state borders Oregon in the south?
California and Nevada

1925. Which river makes up part of the northern boundary of Oregon?
Columbia River

1926. Which river makes up part of the eastern boundary of Oregon?
Snake River

1927. Which body of water borders Oregon in the west?
Pacific Ocean

1928. What is the nickname of Oregon?
Beaver State

1929. What is the state motto of Oregon?
She Flies with Her Own Wings

1930. What is the state song of Oregon?
Oregon, My Oregon

1931. What is the state tree of Oregon?
Douglas Fir

1932. What is the state flower of Oregon?
Oregon Grape

1933. What is the state mushroom of Oregon?
Pacific Golden Chanterelle

1934. What is the state nut of Oregon?
Hazelnut

1935. What is the state bird of Oregon?
Western Meadowlark

1936. What is the state animal of Oregon?
American Beaver

1937. What is the state fish of Oregon?
Chinook Salmon

1938. What is the state insect of Oregon?
Oregon Swallowtail Butterfly

1939. What is the state shell of Oregon?
Oregon Hairy Triton

1940. What is the state rock of Oregon?
Thunдеregg

1941. What is the state gemstone of Oregon?
Oregon Sunstone

1942. What is the state beverage of Oregon?
Milk

1943. What is the state folk dance of Oregon?
Folk Dance

1944. What is the capital of Oregon?
Salem

1945. What is the largest city by population and area in Oregon?
Portland

1946. Who traveled along the Oregon coastlines in 1543?
Bartolome Ferrelo (Spanish explorer)

1947. Who visited Oregon in 1579?
Sir Francis Drake (English captain, privateer, navigator, slaver, and politician)

1948. What was the first permanent white settlement in Oregon, founded in 1811?

Fort Astoria (also named Fort George)

1949. Fort Astoria was the first United States owned settlement on the Pacific coast for 2 years, before who took it over and operated it for 33 years?
British

1950. Following the Anglo American Treaty of 1818, the Oregon region was occupied by which two countries?
United States and Britain

1951. When was the Territory of Oregon established?
August 14th, 1848

1952. When was Oregon admitted to the Union?
February 14th, 1859 (33rd)

1953. What is the area of Oregon?
98,381 sq mi / 255,026 km^2 (9th)

1954. What is the population of Oregon?
3,970,239 (by 2014)

1955. What is the topography of Oregon?
Mountainous in the west; desert in the central and east

1956. What is the highest point of Oregon?
Mount Hood (11,249 ft / 3,429 m)

1957. What is the lowest point of Oregon?
Pacific Ocean (0 ft / 0 m)

1958. How long is the coastline of Oregon?
296 mi / 476 km (8th)

1959. What are the major rivers in Oregon?
Columbia River, Deschutes, Willamette River, John Day River, and Snake River

1960. What are the major lakes in Oregon?
Upper Klamath Lake and Crater Lake

1961. Which bridge, completed in 1966, connects Oregon and Washington?
Astoria Bridge

1962. Which national park is located in Oregon?
Crater Lake National Park (286 sq mi / 741 km^2)

1963. What is the Crater Lake National Park famous for?
The deepest lake in the United States (1,945 ft / 594 m) that lies in the caldera of Mount Mazama formed 7,700 years ago after an eruption

1964. Which canyon in Oregon and Idaho is the deepest canyon in the United States?
Hells Canyon (7,993 ft / 2,436 m)

1965. In which city of Oregon was the D River (440 ft /130 m) listed as the shortest river in the Guinness World Records until 1989?
Lincoln City

1966. What are the Sea Lion Caves in Oregon?
A connected system of sea caves and caverns that open to the Pacific Ocean

1967. Among 9 lighthouses standing along the coastline, which lighthouse is 2 mi (3.2 km) away from Sea Lion Caves?
Heceta Head Light

1968. Which park in Portland of Oregon includes a zoo, forestry museum, arboretum, children's

museum, rose garden, Japanese garden, amphitheatre, memorials, archery range, tennis courts, soccer field, picnic areas, playgrounds, public art, and many acres of wild forest with miles of trails?
Washington Park

1969. What is the Oregon's largest state park, featuring 10 waterfalls and a wide variety of forested hiking trails?
Silver Falls State Park

1970. The world's largest long cabin was built in which city of Oregon in 1905 to honor the Lewis and Clark expedition?
Portland

1971. What is the climate in Oregon?
Mild; wet in the west; dry in the east

1972. What are the natural resources in Oregon?
Dense forests, small deposits of a wide variety of minerals, an abundant supply of water, and fertile soils

1973. What are the natural hazards in Oregon?
Tornados, earth quakes, wildfires, and floods

1974. What are the major industries in Oregon?
Timber, paper products, farming (wheat, cattle), mining (coal), computer equipment, and electronics

Pennsylvania

1975. Which state borders Pennsylvania in the north and northeast?
New York

1976. Which state borders Pennsylvania in the east?
New Jersey

1977. Which states border Pennsylvania in the south and west?
West Virginia

1978. Which states border Pennsylvania in the south?
Maryland and Delaware

1979. Which state borders Pennsylvania in the west?
Ohio

1980. Which river makes up the eastern boundary of Pennsylvania?
Delaware River

1981. Which body of water borders Pennsylvania in the northwest?
Lake Erie

1982. What are the nicknames of Pennsylvania?
Keystone State; Quaker State; Coal State; Oil State; State of Independence

1983. What is the state motto of Pennsylvania?
Virtue, Liberty, and Independence

1984. What is the state song of Pennsylvania?
Pennsylvania

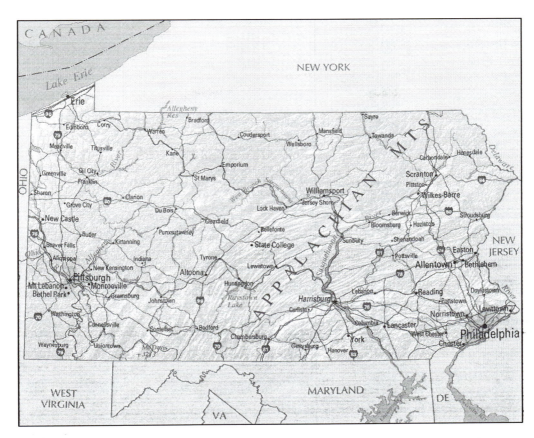

1985. What is the state tree of Pennsylvania?
Eastern Hemlock

1986. What is the state flower of Pennsylvania?
Mountain Laurel

1987. What is the state bird of Pennsylvania?
Ruffed Grouse

1988. What is the state mammal of Pennsylvania?
White-tailed Deer

1989. What are the state insects of Pennsylvania?
Ladybug and Firefly

1990. What is the state dog of Pennsylvania?

Great Dane

1991. What is the state fish of Pennsylvania?
Brook Trout

1992. What is the state fossil of Pennsylvania?
Trilobite

1993. What is the capital of Pennsylvania?
Harrisburg

1994. What is the largest city by population in Pennsylvania?
Philadelphia

1995. What is the largest city by area in Pennsylvania?
Delaware Valley

1996. Who explored Pennsylvania in 1608?
John Smith (British captain)

1997. Who explored Pennsylvania, the area claimed by Dutch in 1609?
Henry Hudson (English navigator and explorer)

1998. Who established the first permanent European settlement in Pennsylvania in 1643, seized by the Swedish in 1655, and by British in 1664?
Johan Printz (New Sweden governor)

1999. Who founded Province of Pennsylvania, a British colony, on March 4th, 1681?
William Penn (English real estate entrepreneur and philosopher)

2000. The Declaration of Independence was signed in which city of Pennsylvania in 1776?
Philadelphia

2001. When was Pennsylvania admitted to the Union?
December 12th, 1787 (2nd)

2002. Which city in Pennsylvania was the temporary capital of the United States during 1790 – 1800?
Philadelphia

2003. What is the area of Pennsylvania?
46,055 sq mi / 119,283 km^2 (33rd)

2004. What is the population of Pennsylvania?
12,787,209 (by 2014)

2005. What is the topography of Pennsylvania?
Mountainous in the southwest to northeast; flat in the east

2006. What is the highest point of Pennsylvania, located in the Allegheny Mountains?
Mount Davis (3,213 ft / 979 m)

2007. What is the lowest point of Pennsylvania?
Delaware River (0 ft / 0 m)

2008. What are the major rivers in Pennsylvania?
Allegheny River, Susquehanna River, Delaware River, and Ohio River

2009. What is the major lake in Pennsylvania?
Lake Erie

2010. Which university in Pennsylvania claims to be America's First University, although it was established in 1740, later than Harvard?
University of Pennsylvania

2011. The first general-purpose electronic computer was announced on February 14th, 1946 by

the University of Pennsylvania, located in which city of Pennsylvania?
Philadelphia
2012. The first daily newspaper was published in which City of Pennsylvania on September 21st, 1784?
Philadelphia
2013. In which city of Pennsylvania did Edwin L. Drake drill the world's first oil well in 1859 and launch the modern petroleum industry?
Titusville
2014. Betsy Ross made the first American flag in which city of Pennsylvania?
Philadelphia
2015. Which bridge in Harrisburg of Pennsylvania is the longest stone arch bridge in the world?
The Rockville Bridge
2016. The Liberty Bell, an iconic symbol of American Independence, is in which city of Pennsylvania?
Philadelphia
2017. Which city in Pennsylvania claims to be the Chocolate Capital of the United States?
Hershey
2018. What is the climate in Pennsylvania?
Continental, humid summers, and cold winters
2019. What are the natural resources in Pennsylvania?
Rich soils, great mineral wealth, good water supplies, and plentiful timber
2020. What are the natural hazards in Pennsylvania?
Hurricanes, tornados, blizzards, and floods
2021. What are the major industries in Pennsylvania?
Steel, farming (corn, oats, soybeans, mushrooms), mining (iron, Portland cement, lime, stone), electronics equipment, cars, and pharmaceuticals

Rhode Island

2022. What is the official name of Rhode Island?
State of Rhode Island and Providence Plantations
2023. Which state borders Rhode Island in the north and east?
Massachusetts
2024. Which state borders Rhode Island in the west?
Connecticut
2025. Which water body lies to the south of Rhode Island?
Atlantic Ocean
2026. Which state has a water border with Rhode Island to the southwest?
New York
2027. What are the nicknames of Rhode Island?
Ocean State; Little Rhody
2028. What is the state motto of Rhode Island?
Hope
2029. What is the state song of Rhode Island?
Rhode Island, It's for Me

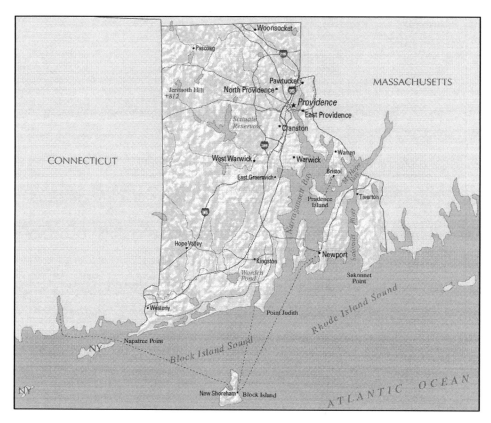

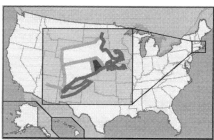

2030. What is the state tree of Rhode Island?
Red Maple

2031. What is the state flower of Rhode Island?
Violets

2032. What is the state bird of Rhode Island?
Rhode Island Red

2033. What is the state shell of Rhode Island?
Quahog

2034. What is the state rock of Rhode Island?
Cumberlandite

2035. What is the state mineral of Rhode Island?
Bowenite

2036. What is the capital of Rhode Island?
Providence (the largest city by population and area)

2037. Who explored the Narragansett Bay and coastal areas of Rhode Island in 1524?
Giovanni da Verrazzano (Italian explorer in the service of French)

2038. Who founded the Colony of Rhode Island and Providence Plantations, a British colony, in 1636?
Roger Williams (English Protestant theologian)

2039. In which city of Rhode Island did Roger Williams found the United States' first Baptist church in 1939?
Providence

2040. When was Rhode Island admitted to the Union?
May 29th, 1790 (13th)

2041. What is the area of Rhode Island?
1,214 sq mi / 3,140 km^2 (50th)

2042. What is the population of Rhode Island?
1,055,173 (by 2014)

2043. What is the topography of Rhode Island?
Flat throughout

2044. What is the highest point of Rhode Island, located in the Appalachian Mountains?
Jerimoth Hill (811 ft / 247 m)

2045. What is the lowest point of Rhode Island?
Atlantic Ocean (0 ft / 0 m)

2046. How long is the coastline of Rhode Island?
40 mi / 64 km (20th)

2047. What is the major river in Rhode Island?
Sakonnet River

2048. What is the major lake in Rhode Island?
Scituate Reservoir

2049. Which suspension bridge connecting the city of Newport on Aquidneck Island and the town of Jamestown on Conanicut Island?
Claiborne Pell Bridge (also called Newport Bridge)

2050. In which city of Rhode Island did the first circus in the United States open in 1774?
Newport

2051. Which library in Newport is the United States' oldest library building?
The Redwood Library and Athenaeum

2052. Which city in Rhode Island is home to the oldest schoolhouse in the United States, built in 1716?
Portsmouth

2053. What is the climate in Rhode Island?
Humid continental, warm summers and cold winters

2054. What are the natural resources in Rhode Island?
Westerly Granite, sand and gravel deposits, and some limestone and sandstone

2055. What are the natural hazards in Rhode Island?
Hurricanes, tornados, and winter storms

2056. What are the major industries in Rhode Island?

South Carolina

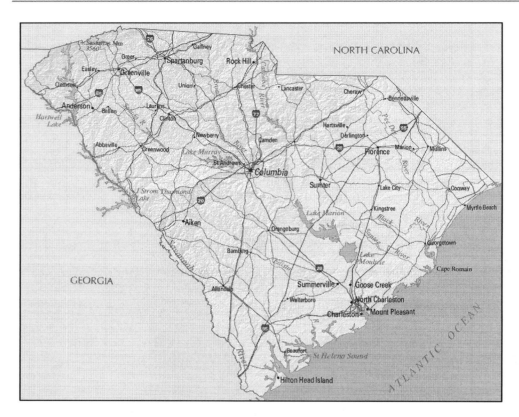

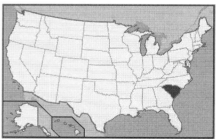

2057. Which state borders South Carolina in the north?
   North Carolina
2058. Which body of water lies to the southeast of South Carolina?
   Atlantic Ocean
2059. Which state borders South Carolina in the south and west?
   Georgia
2060. Which river makes up the southwest boundary of South Carolina?
   Savannah River
2061. What is the nickname of South Carolina?

Palmetto State

2062. What is the state motto of South Carolina?
While I Breathe, I Hope

2063. What is the state song of South Carolina?
Carolina

2064. What is the state tree of South Carolina?
Sabal Palmetto

2065. What is the state flower of South Carolina?
Yellow Jessamine

2066. What is the state fruit of South Carolina?
Peach

2067. What is the state bird of South Carolina?
Carolina Wren

2068. What is the state game bird of South Carolina?
Wild Turkey

2069. What is the state animal of South Carolina?
White-tailed Deer

2070. What is the state butterfly of South Carolina?
Eastern Tiger Swallowtail Butterfly

2071. What is the state insect of South Carolina?
Carolina Mantis

2072. What is the state fish of South Carolina?
Striped Bass

2073. What is the state dog of South Carolina?
Boykin Spaniel

2074. What is the state reptile of South Carolina?
Loggerhead Turtle

2075. What is the state spider of South Carolina?
Carolina Wolf Spider

2076. What is the state amphibian of South Carolina?
Spotted Salamander

2077. What is the state shell of South Carolina?
Lettered Olive

2078. What is the state stone of South Carolina?
Blue Granite

2079. What is the state gemstone of South Carolina?
Amethyst

2080. What is the state soil of South Carolina?
Lynchburg

2081. What is the state beverage of South Carolina?
Milk

2082. What is the state hospitality beverage of South Carolina?
Tea

2083. What is the state dance of South Carolina?
Shag

2084. What is the state folk dance of South Carolina?
Square Dance

2085. What is the state waltz of South Carolina?
Richardson Waltz

2086. What is the capital of South Carolina?
Columbia (the largest city by population and area)

2087. In which year was the Province of Carolina, a British colony, established?
1629

2088. In which year was the city of Charles Towne renamed Charleston, and moved to its present-day location?
1670

2089. In which year was the Province of South Carolina, a British colony, established?
1729

2090. When was South Carolina admitted to the Union?
May 23rd, 1788 (8th)

2091. During which period did South Carolina secede from the Union?
1860 – 1868

2092. What is the area of South Carolina?
32,020 sq mi / 82,931 km^2 (40th)

2093. What is the population of South Carolina?
4,832,482 (by 2014)

2094. What is the topography of South Carolina?
Coastal plains in the southeast; rolling hills in the northwest

2095. What is the highest point of South Carolina, located in the Blue Ridge Mountains?
Sassafras Mountains (3,560 ft / 1,085 m)

2096. What is the lowest point of South Carolina?
Atlantic Ocean (0 ft / 0 m)

2097. How long is the coastline of South Carolina?
187 mi / 301 km (11th)

2098. What are the major rivers in South Carolina?
Santee River, Edisto River, and Savannah River

2099. What are the major lakes in South Carolina?
Lake Marion, Lake Moultrie, Lake Murray, and Hartwell Lake

2100. Which national park is located in South Carolina?
Congaree National Park (41 sq mi / 107 km^2)

2101. What is the Congaree National Park famous for?
The largest portion of old-growth floodplain forest left in North America

2102. Which city in South Carolina is known as the Peach Capital of the World?
Johnston

2103. Which city in South Carolina is South Carolinas' largest tobacco market?
Mullins

2104. Which waterfall is the highest cascade in eastern America, descending nearly 411 feet (125 m)?
The Upper Whitewater Falls

2105. What is the climate in South Carolina?

Humid subtropical; mild winters in the coastal areas; cold winters inland; warm humid summers

2106. What are the natural resources in South Carolina?

Rich soils, minerals (kaolin clay, limestone, peat and sand and gravel, gold, granite, mica, sand, talc, topaz, vermiculite), vast forests (loblolly, pines, oaks, hickories, dogwoods, red maples, slash and longleaf pines, oaks, hickories, magnolias, bay trees, bald cypresses, black tupelos, sweet gums, tulip trees, hemlocks, palmettos), and plentiful water supply

2107. What are the natural hazards in South Carolina?

Hurricanes, tornados, and earthquakes

2108. What are the major industries in South Carolina?

Farming (tobacco, soybeans), textiles, manufacturing chemicals, processed foods, machinery, electronics, paper products, and tourism

South Dakota

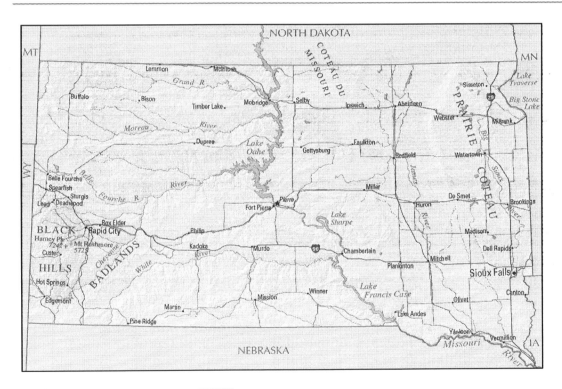

2109. Which state borders South Dakota in the north?
   North Dakota
2110. Which states borders South Dakota in the east?
   Minnesota and Iowa
2111. Which state borders South Dakota in the south?
   Nebraska
2112. Which states border South Dakota in the west?
   Montana and Wyoming
2113. Which rivers make up part of the eastern boundary of South Dakota?
   Big Sioux River
2114. Which rivers make up part of the southern boundary of South Dakota?
   Missouri River
2115. What are the nicknames of South Dakota?
   Mount Rushmore State; Coyote State
2116. What is the state motto of South Dakota?
   Under God the People Rule
2117. What is the state song of South Dakota?
   Hail, South Dakota
2118. What is the state tree of South Dakota?
   Black Hills Spruce
2119. What is the state flower of South Dakota?
   American Pasqueflower
2120. What is the state bird of South Dakota?
   Chinese Ring-necked Pheasant
2121. What is the state mammal of South Dakota?
   Coyote
2122. What is the state fish of South Dakota?
   Walleye
2123. What is the state insect of South Dakota?
   Honeybee
2124. What is the state fossil of South Dakota?
   Triceratops
2125. What is the state mineral of South Dakota?
   Rose Quartz
2126. What is the state gemstone of South Dakota?
   Fairburn Agate
2127. What is the state jewelry of South Dakota?
   Black Hills Gold
2128. What is the state soil of South Dakota?
   Houdek
2129. What is the capital of South Dakota?
   Pierre
2130. What is the largest city by population in South Dakota?
   Sioux Falls
2131. In which year did two sons of Pierre Gaultier de Varennes (French Canadian military officer,

fur trader, and explorer) entered South Dakota, and claimed the area for France?

1743

2132. Nearly all of South Dakota was purchased from France by which treaty signed on April 30th, 1803?

Louisiana Purchase

2133. Who founded the trading post in 1817 at Fort Pierre, the oldest continuous white settlement in South Dakota?

Joseph LaFramboise (American trader and frontiersman)

2134. When was the Territory of Dakota established, splitting from the Territory of Nebraska?

March 2nd, 1861

2135. When was South Dakota admitted to the Union?

November 2nd, 1889 (40th)

2136. What is the area of South Dakota?

77,116 sq mi (199,905 km^2) (17th)

2137. What is the population of South Dakota?

853,175 (by 2014)

2138. What is the topography of South Dakota?

Mainly flat throughout; rolling hills to the west of the Missouri River

2139. What is the highest point of South Dakota, located in the Black Hills?

Harney Peak (7,244 ft / 2,208 m)

2140. What is the lowest point of South Dakota?

Big Stone Lake (968 ft / 295 m)

2141. What are the major rivers in South Dakota?

Cheyenne River, Missouri River, James River, and White River

2142. What are the major lakes in South Dakota?

Lake Oahe, Lake Francis Case, Lake Sharpe, and Lewis and Clark Lake

2143. Which national parks are located in South Dakota?

Badlands National Park (379 sq mi / 982 km^2) and Wind Cave National Park (44 sq mi / 115 km^2)

2144. What is the Badlands National Park famous for?

A collection of buttes, pinnacles, spires, and grass prairies

2145. What is the Wind Cave National Park famous for?

The calcite fin formations called boxwork and the needle-like growths called frostwork

2146. The faces of which four presidents are sculpted into Mount Rushmore?

George Washington, Thomas Jefferson, Theodore Roosevelt, and Abraham Lincoln

2147. Which city in South Dakota contains the geographical center of the United States of America?

Belle Fourche

2148. Which cave in South Dakota is the 2nd longest cave in the world?

Jewel Cave (150 mi / 242 km)

2149. Which city in South Dakota is the home to the Homestake Mine, the largest underground gold mine?

Lead

2150. What is the climate in South Dakota?

Continental; cold and dry winters and warm summers

2151. What are the natural resources in South Dakota?
   Fertile soil and rich mineral resources
2152. What are the natural hazards in South Dakota?
   Tornados, blizzards, and floods
2153. What are the major industries in South Dakota?
   Cattle farming, gold mining, food products, machinery, and wood products

Tennessee

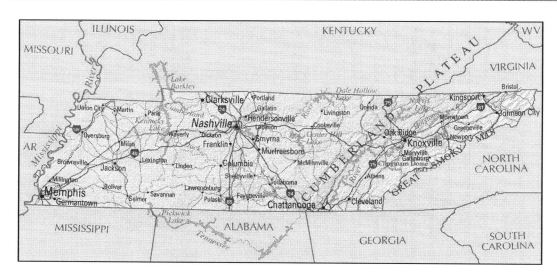

2154. Which states border Tennessee in the north?
   Kentucky and Virginia
2155. Which state borders Tennessee in the east?
   North Carolina
2156. Which states border Tennessee in the south?
   Mississippi, Alabama, and Georgia
2157. Which states border Tennessee in the west?
   Missouri and Arkansas
2158. Which rivers make up the western boundary of Tennessee?
   Mississippi River
2159. What is the nickname of Tennessee?
   Volunteer State

2160. What is the state motto of Tennessee?
Agriculture and Commerce

2161. What are the state songs of Tennessee?
My Homeland Tennessee; The Tennessee Waltz; When It's Iris Time in Tennessee; My Tennessee; Rocky Top; Tennessee; The Pride of Tennessee

2162. What is the state tree of Tennessee?
Tulip Poplar

2163. What is the state flower of Tennessee?
Iris

2164. What is the state wildflower of Tennessee?
Passion Flower

2165. What is the state bird of Tennessee?
Mockingbird

2166. What is the state game bird of Tennessee?
Bobwhite Quail

2167. What is the state wild animal of Tennessee?
Raccoon

2168. What are the state insects of Tennessee?
Firefly and Ladybug

2169. What is the state agriculture insect of Tennessee?
Honeybee

2170. What is the state butterfly of Tennessee?
Zebra Swallowtail

2171. What is the state amphibian of Tennessee?
Tennessee Cave Salamander

2172. What is the state reptile of Tennessee?
Eastern Box Turtle

2173. What is the state sport fish of Tennessee?
Largemouth Bass

2174. What is the state commercial fish of Tennessee?
Channel Catfish

2175. What is the state gemstone of Tennessee?
Tennessee River Pearl

2176. What are the state rocks of Tennessee?
Limestone and Agate

2177. What is the state soil of Tennessee?
Dickson

2178. What is the state dance of Tennessee?
Square Dance

2179. What is the capital of Tennessee?
Nashville

2180. What is the largest city by population in Tennessee?
Memphis

2181. What is the largest city by area in Tennessee?
Nashville

2182. Who explored the Tennessee shore area near Memphis in 1540?
Hernando de Soto (Spanish explorer)

2183. Who claimed the Tennessee area for France in 1682?
Robert de LaSalle (French explorer)

2184. In which year did Britain control Tennessee after the decisive victory of the French and Indian War?
1763

2185. Which town, the oldest permanent settlement in Tennessee, became the first chartered town in 1779?
Jonesboro

2186. When was the Southwest Territory (also called Territory South of the River Ohio) established, split from North Carolina?
May 26th, 1790

2187. When was Tennessee admitted to the Union?
June 1st, 1796 (16th)

2188. During which period did Texas secede from the Union?
1861 – 1866

2189. What is the area of Tennessee?
42,143 sq mi / (109,247 km^2) (36th)

2190. What is the population of Tennessee?
6,549,352 (by 2014)

2191. What is the topography of Tennessee?
Mountainous in the east; flat in the central area; rolling hills in the west

2192. What is the highest point of Tennessee, located in the Great Smoky Mountains?
Clingsmans Dome (6,643 ft / 2025 m)

2193. What is the lowest point of Tennessee?
Mississippi River at Mississippi border (178 ft / 54 m)

2194. What are the major rivers in Tennessee?
Tennessee River, Mississippi River, Cumberland River, Clinch River, and Duck River

2195. What are the major lakes in Tennessee?
Kentucky Lake, Norris Lake, Chickamauga Lake, Cherokee Lake, and Tims Ford Reservoir

2196. Which national park is located in Tennessee?
Great Smoky Mountains National Park (in North Carolina and Tennessee)

2197. The Manhattan Project that produced the first atomic bomb began in which city of Tennessee in 1942?
Oak Ridge

2198. What are the nicknames of Oak Ridge?
Atomic City; Secret City; Energy Capital of the World

2199. Which house in Tennessee was opened to the public on June 7th, 1982 for the memory of Elvis Presley, the King of Rock and Roll?
Graceland Mansion

2200. Which city in Tennessee has the only monument in the United States honoring both the Union and Confederate armies?
Greeneville

2201. Which city in Tennessee is known as the Birthplace of Country Music?

Bristol
2202. The National Civil Rights Museum is at the Lorraine Motel in which city of Tennessee, where Dr. Martin Luther King, Jr. was assassinated in 1968?
Memphis
2203. Which sea in the city of Sweetwater is the largest underground lake in the United States?
Lost Sea
2204. What is the climate in Tennessee?
Humid subtropical; mountain temperate at some of the higher elevations in the Appalachians
2205. What are the natural resources in Tennessee?
Fertile soil, mild climate, huge water systems, and abundant minerals (fluorite, marble, pyrite, zinc, limestone, phosphate rock, coal, small amount of petroleum and natural gas, Ball clay, lignite, sand and gravel, and barite)
2206. What are the natural hazards in Tennessee?
Hurricanes, tornados, earthquakes, floods, and winter storms
2207. What are the major industries in Tennessee?
Mining (coal), electrical power, enriched uranium production, music, automobile manufacturing, farming (tobacco, cattle, soybeans, cotton), walking horses, and tourism

Texas

2208. Which state borders Texas in the north?
Oklahoma
2209. Which state borders Texas in the northeast?
Arkansas
2210. Which state borders Texas in the east?
Louisiana
2211. Which state borders Texas in the northwest?
New Mexico
2212. Which country borders Texas in the southwest?
Mexico
2213. Which river makes up the southwestern boundary of Texas?
Rio Grande
2214. Which rivers make up part of the eastern boundary of Texas?
Sabine River
2215. Which rivers make up part of the northern boundary of Texas?
Red River
2216. Which water body lies to the southeast of Texas?
Gulf of Mexico
2217. What is the nickname of Texas?
Lone Star State
2218. What is the state motto of Texas?
Friendship
2219. What is the state song of Texas?
Texas, Our Texas

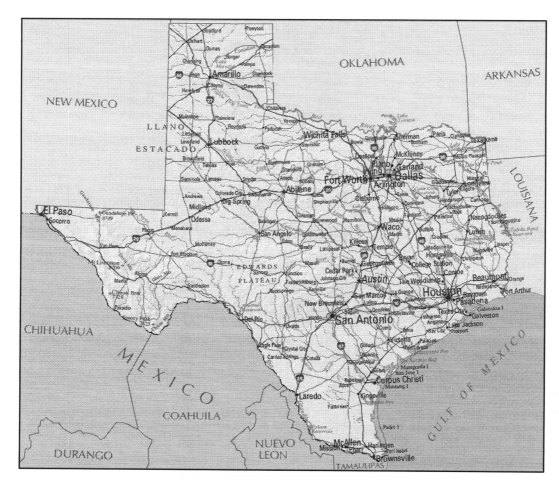

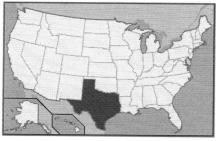

2220. What is the state tree of Texas?
Pecan

2221. What is the state flower of Texas?
Bluebonnet

2222. What is the state plant of Texas?
Prickly Pear Cactus

2223. What is the state grass of Texas?
Sideoats Grama

2224. What is the state shrub of Texas?

Chinese Crepe Myrtle
2225. What is the state fruit of Texas?
Red Grapefruit
2226. What is the vegetable flower of Texas?
Sweet Onion
2227. What is the state fiber of Texas?
Cotton
2228. What is the state bird of Texas?
Mockingbird
2229. What is the state large mammal of Texas?
Texas Longhorn
2230. What is the state small mammal of Texas?
Armadillo
2231. What is the state flying mammal of Texas?
Free-tailed Bat
2232. What is the state insect of Texas?
Monarch Butterfly
2233. What is the state reptile of Texas?
Texas Horned Lizard
2234. What is the state fish of Texas?
Guadalupe Bass
2235. What is the state shell of Texas?
Lightning Whelk
2236. What is the state dinosaur of Texas?
Pleurocoelus
2237. What is the state stone of Texas?
Petrified Palmwood
2238. What is the state gem of Texas?
Texas Blue Topaz
2239. What is the capital of Texas?
Austin
2240. What is the largest city by population in Texas?
Houston
2241. What is the largest city by area in Texas?
Dallas-Fort Worth
2242. Who mapped the Texas coastline in 1519, which became the first document in Texas history?
Alonso Alvarez de Pineda (Spanish explorer)
2243. The first Spanish mission in Texas, Corpus Christi de la Isleta, was established near which present-day city?
El Paso
2244. Who established Fort St. Louis, a French colony, in 1685?
Robert de LaSalle (French explorer)
2245. In which year was Spanish Texas, the interior provinces of New Spain, established?
1690

2246. Northern Texas was purchased from France by which treaty signed on April 30th, 1803?
Louisiana Purchase

2247. In which year did Texas become an integral part of Mexico?
1821

2248. In which year was the Republic of Texas established as a sovereign state including the present-day Texas, and parts of New Mexico, Oklahoma, Kansas, and Colorado?
1836

2249. When was Texas admitted to the Union?
December 29th, 1845 (28th)

2250. During which period did Texas secede from the Union?
1861 – 1870

2251. What is the area of Texas?
268,580 sq mi / 695,621 km^2 (30th)

2252. What is the population of Texas?
26,956,958 (by 2014)

2253. What is the topography of Texas?
Coastal plains in the south and east; flat in the central area; rolling hills in the west

2254. What is the highest point of Texas, located in the Guadalupe Mountains?
Guadeloupe Peak (8,751 ft / 2,667 m)

2255. What is the lowest point of Texas?
Gulf of Mexico (0 ft / 0 m)

2256. How long is the coastline of Texas?
367 mi / 591 km (6th)

2257. What are the major rivers in Texas?
Rio Grande, Red River, and Brazos River

2258. Which lake in Texas is the only natural lake in the state?
Caddo Lake

2259. Which national parks are located in Texas?
Big Bend National Park (1,252 sq mi / 3,242 km^2) and Guadalupe Mountains National Park (135 sq mi / 350 km^2)

2260. What is the Big Bend National Park famous for?
The largest protected area of Chihuahuan Desert with a wide variety of Cretaceous and Tertiary fossils, as well as cultural artifacts of Native Americans

2261. What is the Guadalupe Mountains National Park famous for?
The highest point in Texas; the scenic McKittrick Canyon full of Bigtooth Maples; part of the Chihuahuan Desert; a fossilized reef from the Permian

2262. Which city in Texas claims to be the Live Music Capital of the World?
Austin

2263. The first suspension bridge in the United States, the Waco Bridge (1869), was built to cross which river?
Brazos River

2264. What is the climate in Texas?
Mild winters in the southeast; dry and more extreme seasons in other regions

2265. What are the natural resources in Texas?
Large mineral deposits (petroleum and natural gas), large deposits of sulfur, salt, lignite and

limestone, fertile soils, and rich grasslands

2266. What are the natural hazards in Texas?
Hurricanes, tornados, and wildfires

2267. What are the major industries in Texas?
Petroleum and natural gas, farming (cotton, livestock), steel, banking, insurance, and tourism

Utah

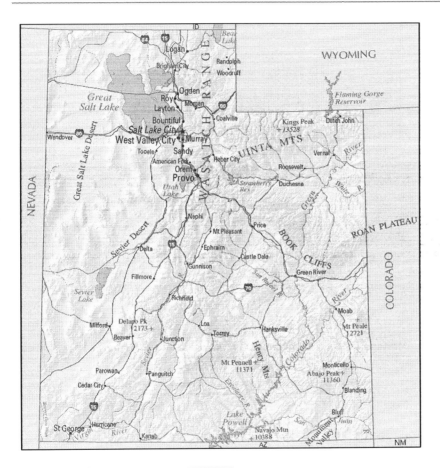

2268. Which state borders Utah in the northeast?

Wyoming
2269. Which state borders Utah in the north?
Idaho
2270. Which state borders Utah in the east?
Colorado
2271. Which state borders Utah in the south?
Arizona
2272. Which state borders Utah in the west?
Nevada
2273. Which state touches Utah in the southeast?
New Mexico
2274. What is the nickname of Utah?
Beehive State
2275. What is the state motto of Utah?
Industry
2276. What is the state song of Utah?
Utah, We Love Thee
2277. What is the state tree of Utah?
Blue Spruce
2278. What is the state flower of Utah?
Sego Lily
2279. What is the state fruit of Utah?
Cherry
2280. What is the state grass of Utah?
Indian Rice Grass
2281. What is the state bird of Utah?
California Sea Gull
2282. What is the state animal of Utah?
Rocky Mountain Elk
2283. What is the state fish of Utah?
Bonneville Cutthroat Trout
2284. What is the state insect of Utah?
Honeybee
2285. What is the state fossil of Utah?
Allosaurus
2286. What is the state rock of Utah?
Coal
2287. What is the state mineral of Utah?
Copper
2288. What is the state gem of Utah?
Topaz
2289. What is the state emblem of Utah?
Beehive
2290. What is the state dance of Utah?
Square Dance

2291. What is the state cooking pot of Utah?
Dutch Oven
2292. What is the capital of Utah?
Salt Lake City (the largest city by population and area)
2293. Who explored Utah on the way to California in 1776?
Silvestre Velez de Escalante and Francesco Atanasio Dominguez (Spanish priests)
2294. Who claimed all of Utah in 1821?
Mexico
2295. When did Brigham Young and Mormon pioneers arrive in Salt Lake Valley?
July 24th, 1847
2296. By which treaty was Utah granted to the United States in 1848?
Treaty of Guadalupe Hidalgo
2297. When was the Territory of Utah established?
September 9th, 1850
2298. When was Utah admitted to the Union?
January 4th, 1896 (45th)
2299. What was the Utah War during March 1857 – July 1858?
An armed confrontation between Mormon pioneers in the Utah Territory and the armed forces of the United States government
2300. What is the area of Utah?
84,899 sq mi / 219,887 km^2 (13th)
2301. What is the population of Utah?
2,942,902 (by 2014)
2302. What is the topography of Utah?
Mostly mountainous with flat areas
2303. What is the highest point of Utah, located in the Uinta Mountains?
Kings Peak (13,518 ft / 4,120 m)
2304. What is the lowest point of Utah?
Beaver Dam Wash at Arizona border (2,180 ft / 664 m)
2305. What are the major rivers in Utah?
Colorado River and Green River
2306. What are the major lakes in Utah?
Great Salt Lake, Lake Powell, and Utah Lake
2307. Which national parks are located in Utah?
Arches National Park (120 sq mi / 310 km^2), Bryce Canyon National Park (56 sq mi / 145 km^2), Canyonlands National Park (527 sq mi / 1,366 km^2), Capitol Reef National Park (378 sq mi / 979 km^2), and Zion National Park (229 sq mi / 593 km^2)
2308. What is the Arches National Park famous for?
More than 2,000 natural sandstone arches, including the Delicate Arch
2309. What is the Bryce Canyon National Park famous for?
A giant natural amphitheatre along the Paunsaugunt Plateau
2310. What is the Canyonlands National Park famous for?
A colorful landscape eroded into countless canyons, mesas, and buttes
2311. What is the Capitol Reef National Park famous for?
Colorful canyons, ridges, buttes, and monoliths; about 75 mi (120 km) of a rugged spine

extending from Thousand Lake Mountain to Lake Powell called the Waterpocket Fold

2312. What is the Zion National Park famous for?
Colorful sandstone canyons, high plateaus, and rock towers

2313. Which sandstone structure in Utah is the world's largest natural-rock span?
Rainbow Bridge

2314. What is the nickname of Salt Lake City?
Crossroads of the West

2315. Which city in Utah, known as Little Hollywood, is situated in the Grand Circle area, centrally located among Bryce Canyon National Park, the Grand Canyon (North Rim), Zion National Park, and Lake Powell?
Kanab

2316. Which lake in Utah is about 75 miles (121 km) long and 35 miles (56 km) wide, covers 1,700 sq mi (4,400 km²), and is the 4th largest terminal lake in the world?
Great Salt Lake

2317. The United States' Transcontinental Railroad was completed at which location in Utah, where the Central Pacific and Union Pacific Railroads met, on May 10th, 1869?
Promontory

2318. What is the climate in Utah?
Dry, semi-arid to desert

2319. What are the natural resources in Utah?
Coal, petroleum, natural gas, uranium, copper, gold, molybdenum, silver, magnesium, and salts

2320. What are the natural hazards in Utah?
Tornados, wildfires, winter storms, and earthquakes

2321. What are the major industries in Utah?
Oil, natural gas, mining (coal, copper, iron ore, silver, gold), steel-making, farming (cattle, sheep, dairy products), and tourism (especially skiing)

Vermont

2322. Which state borders Vermont in the east?
New Hampshire

2323. Which state borders Vermont in the south?
Massachusetts

2324. Which state borders Vermont in the west?
New York

2325. Which country borders Vermont in the north?
Canada

2326. Which river makes up the eastern boundary of Vermont?
Connecticut River

2327. Which water body lies to the west of Vermont?
Lake Champlain

2328. What is the nickname of Vermont?
Green Mountain State

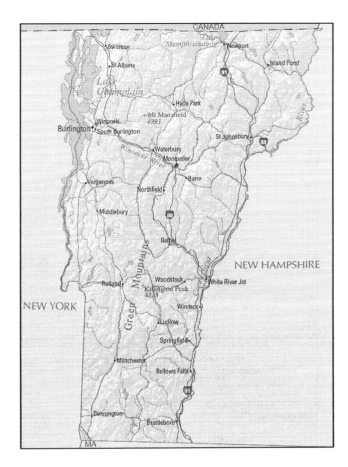

2329. What is the state motto of Vermont?
Freedom and Unity

2330. What is the state song of Vermont?
These Green Mountains

2331. What is the state tree of Vermont?
Sugar Maple

2332. What is the state flower of Vermont?
Red Clover

2333. What is the state bird of Vermont?
Hermit Thrush

2334. What is the state animal of Vermont?
Morgan Horse

2335. What is the state butterfly of Vermont?
Monarch Butterfly

2336. What is the state insect of Vermont?
Honeybee

2337. What is the state cold water fish of Vermont?
Brook Trout

2338. What is the state warm water fish of Vermont?

Walleye

2339. What is the state amphibian of Vermont?
Northern Leopard Frog

2340. What are the state rocks of Vermont?
Granite, Marble, and Slate

2341. What are the state minerals of Vermont?
Talc and Grossular Garnet

2342. What is the capital of Vermont?
Montpelier

2343. What is the largest city by population in Vermont?
Burlington

2344. What is the largest city by area in Vermont?
South Burlington

2345. Who claimed the Lake Champlain area, including Vermont, for France in 1609?
Samuel de Champlain (French explorer)

2346. What was the first European (French) settlement in Vermont, founded on Isle La Motte in 1666?
Fort Sainte Anne

2347. What was the first permanent European (English) settlement in Vermont, founded in 1724?
Fort Drummer

2348. When was the Vermont Republic established?
January 15th, 1777

2349. What was the oldest city in Vermont, incorporated in 1788?
Vergennes

2350. When was Vermont admitted to the Union?
March 4th, 1791 (14th)

2351. What is the area of Vermont?
9,620 sq mi / 24,923 km^2 (45th)

2352. What is the population of Vermont?
626,562 (by 2014)

2353. What is the topography of Vermont?
Mostly mountainous

2354. What is the highest point of Vermont, located in the Green Mountains?
Mount Mansfield (4,395 ft / 1,340 m)

2355. What is the lowest point of Vermont?
Lake Champlain (95 ft / 29 m)

2356. What are the major rivers in Vermont?
Connecticut River, West River, and Otter River

2357. What are the major lakes in Vermont?
Lake Champlain and Lake Memphremagog

2358. Which city is the largest producer of maple syrup in the United States?
Montpelier

2359. Vermont was, at various times, claimed by which states?
New Hampshire and New York

2360. What is the climate in Vermont?

Humid continental

2361. What are the natural resources in Vermont?
Valuable mineral sources, fertile soil, and forests that cover about 4/5 of the state

2362. What are the natural hazards in Vermont?
Hurricanes and winter storms

2363. What are the major industries in Vermont?
Maple syrup, farming (dairy), tourism, electronics, and forest products (especially paper)

Virginia

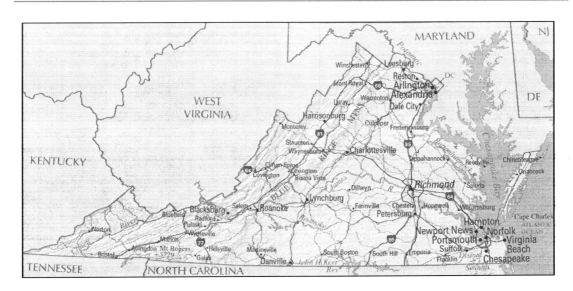

2364. Which state borders Virginia in the northeast?
Maryland

2365. Which state borders Virginia in the north and west?
West Virginia

2366. Which state borders Virginia in the west?
Kentucky

2367. Which states border Virginia in the south?
North Carolina and Tennessee

2368. District of Columbia is between Virginia and which other state?
Maryland

2369. Which water body lies to the east of Virginia?
Atlantic Ocean
2370. The Chesapeake Bay is the largest estuary in the United States, surrounded by Virginia and which state?
Maryland
2371. What are the nicknames of Virginia?
Old Dominion; Mother of Presidents; Mother of states
2372. What is the state motto of Virginia?
Thus Always to Tyrants
2373. What is the state song of Virginia?
Carry Me Back to Old Virginia
2374. What is the state tree of Virginia?
American Dogwood
2375. What is the state flower of Virginia?
American Dogwood
2376. What is the state bird of Virginia?
Cardinal
2377. What is the state dog of Virginia?
American Fox Hound
2378. What is the state insect of Virginia?
Tiger Swallowtail Butterfly
2379. What is the state fish of Virginia?
Brook Trout
2380. What is the state shell of Virginia?
Oyster
2381. What is the state fossil of Virginia?
Chesapecten Jeffersonius
2382. What is the state beverage of Virginia?
Milk
2383. What is the state boat of Virginia?
Chesapeake Bay Deadrise (a type of traditional fishing boat that is used for fishing, crabbing, and oystering)
2384. What is the state dance of Virginia?
Square Dance
2385. What is the capital of Virginia?
Richmond
2386. What is the largest city by population and area in Virginia?
Virginia Beach
2387. What was the oldest permanent English settlement in North America, founded on May 14th, 1607?
Jamestown (the 2nd oldest continuously inhabited city in the United States)
2388. In which year was the Colony of Virginia, the first British colony in North America, established?
1607
2389. In which year was the first Thanksgiving in North America held in Virginia?

1619

2390. When was Virginia admitted to the Union?
June 25th, 1788 (10th)

2391. During which period did Virginia secede from the Union?
1861 – 1870

2392. What is the area of Virginia?
42,774 sq mi / 110,786 km^2 (35th)

2393. What is the population of Virginia?
8,326,289(by 2014)

2394. What is the topography of Virginia?
Mountainous in the west; coastal plains in the east

2395. What is the highest point of Virginia, located in the Blue Ridge Mountains?
Mount Rogers (5,729 ft / 1,746 m)

2396. What is the lowest point of Virginia?
Atlantic Ocean (0 ft / 0 m)

2397. How long is the coastline of Virginia?
112 mi / 180 km (15th)

2398. What are the major rivers in Virginia?
James River, Rappahannock River, Potomac River, and Shenandoah River

2399. What are the major lakes in Virginia?
Atlantic Intracoastal Waterway, Gathright Dam (Lake Moomaw), John H. Kerr Reservoir, John W. Flannagan Reservoir, Pound Lake, and Philpott Lake

2400. Which national park is located in Virginia?
Shenandoah National Park (311 sq mi / 806 km^2)

2401. What is the Shenandoah National Park famous for?
Part of the Blue Ridge Mountains covered by hardwood forests that are home to tens of thousands of animals; the Skyline Drive and Appalachian Trail; scenic overlooks and waterfalls of the Shenandoah River

2402. What is the Historic Triangle in Virginia?
The area including the colonial communities of Jamestown, Colonial Williamsburg, and Yorktown

2403. Which university in Virginia is the oldest public university in the United States, although it was founded in 1693 as a private college and became public in 1906?
The College of William & Mary

2404. What were two capitals of the Colony of Virginia?
Jamestown (1607 – 1699) and Williamsburg (1699 – 1776)

2405. Patrick Henry's "Give me liberty or give me death" speech in 1775 was occurred at St. John's Church in which city of Virginia?
Richmond

2406. Thomas Jefferson's "The Virginia Statute for Religious Freedom" passage in 1777 was drafted in which city of Virginia?
Fredericksburg

2407. The American Revolution ended with the surrender of British General Charles Cornwallis in which town of Virginia on October 9th, 1781?
Yorktown

2408. What are the nicknames of Richmond?

RVA; River City

2409. What are the nicknames of Virginia Beach?

Resort City; Neptune City

2410. Where did the Confederate Army under Robert E. Lee surrender to the Union commander Ulysses S. Grant on April 9th, 1865, effectively ending the American Civil War?

Appomattox Court House

2411. What is the major cash crop of Virginia?

Tobacco

2412. What is the climate in Virginia?

Humid continental; warmer in the southeast region

2413. What are the natural resources in Virginia?

A variety of soil types (from stony and not very fertile to loamy and easily cultivated sandy soils) and many mineral deposits (bituminous and anthracite coal, basalt, dolostone, gneiss, granite, limestone, marble, sandstone, shale, slate, and soapstone)

2414. What are the natural hazards in Virginia?

Hurricanes, tornados, earthquakes, and winter storms

2415. What are the major industries in Virginia?

Farming (tobacco, peanuts, corn, sweet potatoes, poultry, ham), tourism, US Navy warships, mining (coal), lumber (for paper and furniture), and government workers

Washington

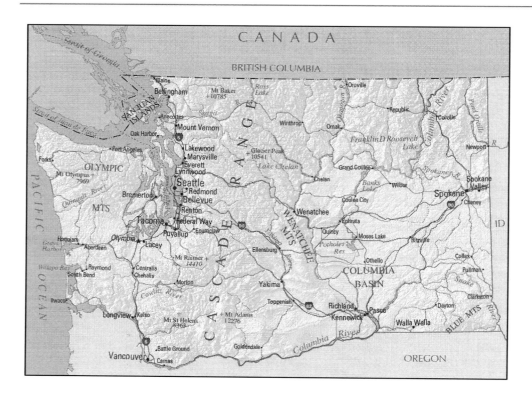

2416. Which state borders Washington in the east?
Idaho

2417. Which state borders Washington in the south?
Oregon

2418. Which country borders Washington in the north?
Canada

2419. Which river makes up part of the southern boundary of Washington?
Columbia River

2420. Which river makes up part of the eastern boundary of Washington?
Snake River

2421. Which water body lies to the west of Washington?
Pacific Ocean

2422. What is the nickname of Washington?
Evergreen State

2423. What is the state motto of Washington?
By and By

2424. What is the state song of Washington?
Washington, My Home

2425. What is the state tree of Washington?
Western Hemlock

2426. What is the state flower of Washington?
Coast Rhododendron

2427. What is the state fruit of Washington?
Apple

2428. What is the state vegetable of Washington?
Walla Walla Sweet Onion

2429. What is the state grass of Washington?
Bluebunch Wheatgrass

2430. What is the state bird of Washington?
Goldfinch

2431. What is the state insect of Washington?
Green Darner Dragonfly

2432. What is the state fish of Washington?
Steelhead Trout

2433. What is the state fossil of Washington?
Columbian Mammoth

2434. What is the state gem of Washington?
Petrified Wood
2435. What is the state ship of Washington?
President Washington
2436. What is the state dance of Washington?
Square Dance
2437. What is the capital of Washington?
Olympia
2438. What is the largest city by population and area in Washington?
Seattle
2439. Who traveled along the Washington coastline in 1543?
Bartolome Ferrelo (Spanish explorer)
2440. Who visited Washington in 1579?
Sir Francis Drake (English captain, privateer, navigator, slaver, and politician)
2441. What was the first settlement in Washington, founded in 1846?
New Market (the present-day Tumwater)
2442. What was the oldest town in Washington, founded in 1851 by Lafayette Balch (American captain) and incorporated in 1854?
Steilacoom
2443. When was the Territory of Washington established, split from the Territory of Oregon?
February 8th, 1853
2444. When was Washington admitted to the Union?
November 11th, 1889 (42nd)
2445. What is the area of Washington?
71,300 sq mi / 184,827 km^2 (18th)
2446. What is the population of Washington?
7,061,530 (by 2014)
2447. What is the topography of Washington?
Mountainous where the Cascade Range crosses Washington; relatively flat elsewhere
2448. What is the highest point of Washington, located in the Cascade Range?
Mount Rainier (14,417 ft / 4,394 m)
2449. What is the lowest point of Washington?
Pacific Ocean (0 ft / 0 m)
2450. How long is the coastline of Washington?
157 mi / 253 km (12th)
2451. What are the major rivers in Washington?
Columbia River, Snake River, and Yakima River
2452. What are the major lakes in Washington?
Lake Franklin D. Roosevelt and Lake Washington
2453. Which national parks are located in Washington?
Mount Rainier National Park (368 sq mi / 954 km^2), North Cascades National Park (789 sq mi /2,043 km^2), and Olympic National Park (1,442 sq mi / 3,734 km^2)
2454. What is the Mount Rainier National Park famous for?
An active volcano, covered by 26 named glaciers including Emmons Glacier, the largest in the 48 contiguous United States

2455. What is the North Cascades National Park famous for?
Numerous glaciers and rugged mountain peaks
2456. What is the Olympic National Park famous for?
The Pacific coastline, alpine areas, the west side temperate rainforest, and the forests of the drier east side
2457. Which area in Washington has the only rainforest in the 48 contiguous United States?
Olympic Peninsula
2458. Washington is home to which four of the five longest floating bridges in the world?
Evergreen Point Floating Bridge (1st, over Lake Washington), Lacey V. Murrow Memorial Bridge (2nd, over Lake Washington), Homer M. Hadley Bridge (3rd, over Lake Washington), and Hood Canal Bridge (5th, connecting the Olympic Peninsula and the Kitsap Peninsula)
2459. Starbucks, the biggest coffee chain in the world, was founded in which city of Washington on March 30th, 1971?
Seattle
2460. What is the climate in Washington?
Oceanic climate in the west; semi-arid east of the Cascade Range; Olympic Peninsula receives is the wettest area of the 48 contiguous United States
2461. What are the natural resources in Washington?
Large supplies of water, large reserves of timber, and fertile soil
2462. What are the natural hazards in Washington?
Volcanoes, earthquakes, wildfires, and tornados
2463. What are the major industries in Washington?
Farming (fruit, berries, nuts, cattle, wheat), lumber, tourism, hydroelectric power, computer software, aircraft, and aluminum refining

West Virginia

2464. Which states border West Virginia in the northeast?
Pennsylvania and Maryland
2465. Which state borders West Virginia in the northwest?
Ohio
2466. Which state borders West Virginia in the south and southeast?
Virginia
2467. Which state borders West Virginia in the southwest?
Kentucky
2468. Which river makes up the western boundary of West Virginia?
Ohio River
2469. Which river makes up part of the northern boundary of West Virginia?
Potomac River
2470. What is the nickname of West Virginia?
Mountain State
2471. What is the state motto of West Virginia?
Mountaineers Are Always Free
2472. What are the state slogans of West Virginia?
Wild and Wonderful; Open for Business; Almost Heaven

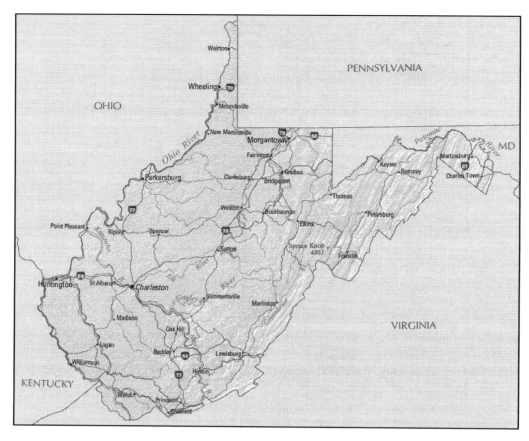

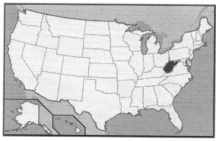

2473. What are the state songs of West Virginia?
West Virginia My Home; The West Virginia Hills; This Is My West Virginia

2474. What is the state tree of West Virginia?
Sugar Maple

2475. What is the state flower of West Virginia?
Rhododendron

2476. What is the state wildflower of West Virginia?
Fringed Gentian

2477. What is the state fruit of West Virginia?
Golden Delicious Apple

2478. What is the state bird of West Virginia?

Northern Cardinal
2479. What is the state animal of West Virginia?
Black Bear
2480. What is the state reptile of West Virginia?
Timber Rattler
2481. What is the state fish of West Virginia?
Brook Trout
2482. What is the state insect of West Virginia?
European Honeybee
2483. What is the state butterfly of West Virginia?
Monarch Butterfly
2484. What is the state gemstone of West Virginia?
Silicified Mississippian Fossil Coral
2485. What is the state rock of West Virginia?
Coal
2486. What is the state soil of West Virginia?
Monongahela Silt Loam
2487. What are the state colors of West Virginia?
Old Gold and Blue
2488. What is the capital of West Virginia?
Charleston (the largest city by population and area)
2489. Which town was the first permanent European settlement in West Virginia, founded in 1732?
Shepherdstown
2490. Why did West Virginia separate from Virginia in 1861?
Because it refused to secede from the Union
2491. When was West Virginia admitted to the Union?
June 20th, 1863 (35th)
2492. What is the area of West Virginia?
24,230 sq mi / 62,755 km^2 (41st)
2493. What is the population of West Virginia?
1,850,326 (by 2014)
2494. What is the topography of West Virginia?
Mountainous throughout
2495. What is the highest point of West Virginia, located in the Appalachian Mountains?
Spruce Knob (summit of the Spruce Mountain, 4,863 ft / 1,482 m)
2496. What is the lowest point of West Virginia?
Potomac River at Virginia border (240 ft / 73 m)
2497. What are the major rivers in West Virginia?
Ohio River, Guyandotte River, and Greenbrier River
2498. What are the major lakes in West Virginia?
Tygart Lake and Bluestone Lake
2499. What are the nicknames of Charleston?
Home of Hospitality; The most northern city of the South; The most southern city of the North; Chemical Valley; The Capital City; Chucktown; Charly West

2500. Mother's Day was first observed at Andrews Church in which city of West Virginia on May 10th, 1908?
Grafton
2501. West Virginia was the first state to have a sales tax. When was it effective?
July 1st, 1921
2502. Which city in West Virginia is home to the Coal House, world's only residence built entirely of coal and occupied on June 1st, 1961?
White Sulphur Springs
2503. Which bridge in West Virginia is the 2nd highest (876 ft / 267 m) and the longest (1,700 ft / 518 m) steel arch bridge in the United States?
New River Gorge Bridge
2504. What is the climate in West Virginia?
Humid subtropical in the south; humid continental in the center and north
2505. What are the natural resources in West Virginia?
Mineral deposits (Coal, natural gas, petroleum, brine and rock salt, limestone, sand, clay, sandstone and shale), timber, and abundant rainfall
2506. What are the natural hazards in West Virginia?
Hurricanes, tornados, and winter storms
2507. What are the major industries in West Virginia?
Mining (coal), livestock, chemical manufacturing, glass products, and tourism

Wisconsin

2508. Which state borders Wisconsin in the northeast?
Michigan
2509. Which state borders Wisconsin in the southwest?
Iowa
2510. Which state borders Wisconsin in the south?
Illinois
2511. Which state borders Wisconsin in the west?
Minnesota
2512. Which rivers make up most of the western boundary of Wisconsin?
Mississippi River and St. Croix River
2513. Which river makes up the northeastern boundary of Wisconsin?
Menominee River
2514. Which water body lies to the north of Wisconsin?
Lake Superior
2515. Which water body lies to the east of Wisconsin?
Lake Michigan
2516. What are the nicknames of Wisconsin?
Badger State; America's Dairyland
2517. What is the state motto of Wisconsin?
Forward
2518. What is the state song of Wisconsin?
On, Wisconsin!

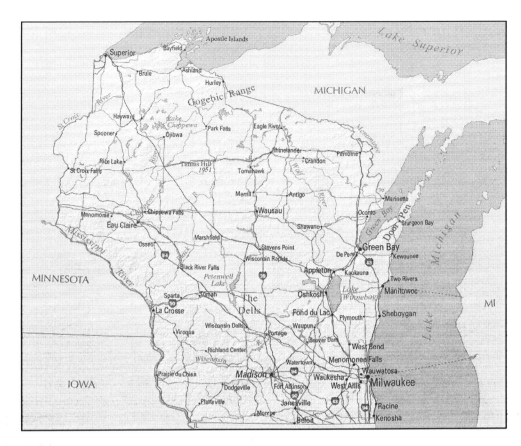

2519. What is the state tree of Wisconsin?
Sugar Maple

2520. What is the state flower of Wisconsin?
Wood Violet

2521. What is the state grain of Wisconsin?
Corn

2522. What is the state bird of Wisconsin?
Robin

2523. What is the state animal of Wisconsin?
Badger

2524. What is the state wildlife animal of Wisconsin?

White-tailed Deer

2525. What is the state domestic animal of Wisconsin?
Dairy Cow

2526. What is the state dog of Wisconsin?
American Water Spaniel

2527. What is the state fish of Wisconsin?
Muskellunge

2528. What is the state insect of Wisconsin?
Honeybee

2529. What is the state symbol of peace of Wisconsin?
Mourning Dove

2530. What is the state fossil of Wisconsin?
Trilobite

2531. What is the state stone of Wisconsin?
Red Granite

2532. What is the state mineral of Wisconsin?
Galena

2533. What is the state soil of Wisconsin?
Antigo Silt Loam

2534. What is the state beverage of Wisconsin?
Milk

2535. What is the state dance of Wisconsin?
Polka

2536. What is the capital of Wisconsin?
Madison

2537. What is the largest city by population and area in Wisconsin?
Milwaukee

2538. Who explored the Green Bay area in 1634?
Jean Nicolet (French explorer)

2539. Jean Nicolet established which trading post in 1634 that making Green Bay the oldest European (French) permanent settlement in Wisconsin?
La Baye

2540. Who explored the upper Mississippi River, including Wisconsin, in 1673?
Jacques Marquette (French explorer) and Louis Jolliet (French missionary)

2541. The Green Bay settlement was established by Augustin Monet de Langlade and Charles Langlade (son of Augustin Monet de Langlade) in 1745. Which one permanently moved to Green Bay in 1764 to become the Father of Wisconsin?
Charles Langlade (fur trader with French Canadian and Ottawa heritage)

2542. Who took control of Green Bay in 1761 and gained control of all of Wisconsin in 1763?
British

2543. When was the Territory Northwest of the River Ohio, including Wisconsin, established?
July 13th, 1787

2544. When was the Territory of Indiana, including Wisconsin, established?
July 4th, 1800

2545. When was the Territory of Illinois, including Wisconsin, split from the Territory of Indiana?

March 1st, 1809

2546. As Illinois was about to become a state in 1818, Wisconsin was joined to which territory?
Territory of Michigan

2547. When was the Territory of Wisconsin split from the Territory of Michigan?
July 3rd, 1836

2548. When was Wisconsin admitted to the Union?
May 29th, 1848 (30th)

2549. What is the area of Wisconsin?
65,498 sq mi / 169,639 km^2 (23rd)

2550. What is the population of Wisconsin?
5,757,564 (by 2014)

2551. What is the topography of Wisconsin?
Flat in the east, center, and north; hills and ridges in the north and west

2552. What is the highest point of Wisconsin, located in the Appalachian Mountains?
Timms Hill (1,951 ft / 595 m)

2553. What is the lowest point of Wisconsin?
Lake Michigan (579 ft / 176 m)

2554. What are the major rivers in Wisconsin?
Wisconsin River, Mississippi River, St. Croix River, and Chippewa River

2555. What are the major lakes in Wisconsin?
Lake Michigan, Lake Superior, and Lake Winnebago

2556. What are the nicknames of Milwaukee?
Cream City; Brew City; Beer City; Brew Town; Beertown; The Mil; MKE; City of Festivals; Deutsch-Athen

2557. Which city in Wisconsin claims to be the Ginseng Capital of the World?
Wausau

2558. Which city in Wisconsin claims to the Bratwurst Capital of the World?
Sheboygan

2559. Which town in Wisconsin claims to be the Loon Capital of the World?
Mercer

2560. What is the climate in Wisconsin?
Humid continental

2561. What are the natural resources in Wisconsin?
Rich soils, minerals, large forest stands, and abundant supplies of water

2562. What are the natural hazards in Wisconsin?
Tornados, wildfires, floods, and winter storms

2563. What are the major industries in Wisconsin?
Dairy products (milk, butter, cheese), farming (corn), machinery, paper manufacturing, beer, and tourism

Wyoming

2564. Which state borders Wyoming in the north and northwest?
Montana

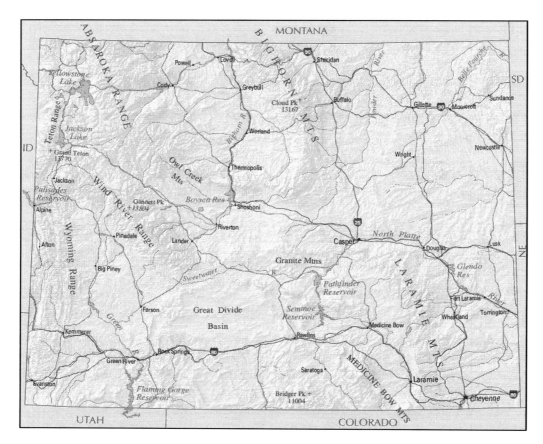

2565. Which states border Wyoming in the east?
South Dakota and Nebraska

2566. Which state borders Wyoming in the southwest?
Utah

2567. Which state borders Wyoming in the south?
Colorado

2568. Which state borders Wyoming in the west?
Idaho

2569. What are the nicknames of Wyoming?
Equality State; Cowboy State; Big Wyoming

2570. What is the state motto of Wyoming?

Equal Rights
2571. What is the state song of Wyoming?
Wyoming
2572. What is the state tree of Wyoming?
Plains Cottonwood
2573. What is the state flower of Wyoming?
Indian Paintbrush
2574. What is the state grass of Wyoming?
Western Wheatgrass
2575. What is the state bird of Wyoming?
Western Meadowlark
2576. What is the state mammal of Wyoming?
Buffalo
2577. What is the state reptile of Wyoming?
Horned Lizard
2578. What is the state fish of Wyoming?
Cutthroat Trout
2579. What is the state dinosaur of Wyoming?
Triceratops
2580. What is the state fossil of Wyoming?
Knightia
2581. What is the state gemstone of Wyoming?
Jade
2582. What is the capital of Wyoming?
Cheyenne (the largest city by population and area)
2583. Who explored Wyoming and discovered Big Horn Mountains during 1742 – 1743?
Two sons of Pierre Gaultier de Varennes (French Canadian military officer)
2584. A Portion of Wyoming was purchased from France by which treaty signed on April 30th, 1803?
Louisiana Purchase
2585. What was the first permanent trading post, founded by William Sublette (American fur trapper, pioneer, and mountain man) in 1834?
Fort Laramie
2586. When was the Territory of Wyoming established?
July 25th, 1868
2587. When was Wyoming admitted to the Union?
July 10th, 1890 (44th)
2588. What is the area of Wyoming?
97,814 sq mi / 253,348 km^2 (10th)
2589. What is the population of Wyoming?
584,153 (by 2014)
2590. What is the topography of Wyoming?
The western two thirds of the state is covered mostly with the mountain ranges and rangelands in the foothills of the Eastern Rocky Mountains; the eastern third of the state is high elevation prairie known as the High Plains, and the continental divide

2591. What is the highest point of Wyoming, located in the Wind River Range?
Gannett Peak (13,809 ft / 4,209 m)
2592. What is the lowest point of Wyoming?
Belle Fourche River at South Dakota border (3,101 ft / 945 m)
2593. What are the major rivers in Wyoming?
Bighorn River, Green River, Belle Fourche River, Powder River, and North Platte River
2594. What are the major lakes in Wyoming?
Yellowstone Lake, Glendo Reservoir, Bighorn Lake, Boysen Reservoir, Flaming Gorge Reservoir, Seminole Reservoir, Alcova Reservoir, and Keyhole Reservoir
2595. Which national parks are located in Wyoming?
Grand Teton National Park (484 sq mi / 1,255 km^2) and Yellowstone National Park (in Wyoming, Montana, and Idaho, 3,472 sq mi / 8,987 km^2)
2596. What is the Grand Teton National Park famous for?
Jackson Hole valley and reflective piedmont lakes contrast with the tall mountains that abruptly rise from the glacial sage-covered valley
2597. What is the Yellowstone National Park famous for?
World's first national park (March 1st, 1872); vast geothermal areas such as hot springs and geysers, the best-known being Old Faithful Geyser and Grand Prismatic Spring
2598. What was designated as the first National Monument in the United States on September 24th, 1906?
Devils Tower
2599. Which surface coal mine in Wyoming contains one of the largest deposits of coal in the world?
Black Thunder Coal Mine
2600. What is the climate in Wyoming?
Semi-arid and continental
2601. What are the natural resources in Wyoming?
Mineral deposits (bentonite clay, coal, petroleum, sodium carbonate, uranium, agate, jade, gold), grazing land, beautiful scenery, wildlife and water
2602. What are the natural hazards in Wyoming?
Tornados, wildfires, and earthquakes
2603. What are the major industries in Wyoming?
Farming (cattle, sheep), mining (coal, uranium), oil, natural gas, and tourism

Miscellaneous

2604. What is the area of the United States?
3,794,101 sq mi / 9,826,675 km^2

2605. What is the population of the United States?
318,857,056 (by 2014)

2606. What is the highest point of the United States?
Mount McKinley (20,320 ft / 6,194 m)

2607. What is the lowest point of the United States?
Badwater Basin in Death Valley (-282 ft / -86 m)

2608. Which national park is located in American Samoa?
American Samoa National Park (14 sq mi / 36 km^2)

2609. What is the American Samoa National Park famous for?
Coral reefs, rainforests, volcanic mountains, and white beaches

2610. Which national park is located in Virgin Islands?
Virgin Islands National Park (23 sq mi / 59 km^2)

2611. What is the Virgin Islands National Park famous for?
Taino archaeological sites and ruins of sugar plantations from Columbus's time; mangroves, seagrass beds, coral reefs and algal plains

2612. What is Tornado Alley?
A region between the Rocky and Appalachian Mountains where there are the most tornadoes in the world

2613. At the Four Corners, a person can stand in four states at the same time. Which four states are they?
Colorado, Arizona, New Mexico, and Utah

2614. Which four states in the United States are constituted a commonwealth?
Kentucky, Virginia, Pennsylvania, and Massachusetts

2615. What was New Netherland?
A 17th century Dutch colony in the Mid-Atlantic United States

2616. Which modern states belonged to New Netherland?
New York, New Jersey, Delaware, and Connecticut

2617. What were the Thirteen Colonies?
British colonies (present-day Delaware, Pennsylvania, New Jersey, Georgia, Connecticut, Massachusetts, Maryland, South Carolina, New Hampshire, Virginia, New York, North Carolina, and Rhode Island) that gained independence through the American Revolutionary War

2618. When did the American Revolutionary War officially start?
April 19th, 1775

2619. In which city of New Hampshire was the first shot of the American Revolutionary War fired?
Concord

2620. Which country was the United States fighting against in the American Revolutionary War?
The United Kingdom

2621. Which country first provided military aid to the United States in the American Revolutionary War?

France
2622. What day did the United States sign the Declaration of Independence?
July 4th, 1776

2623. When did the American Revolutionary War end?
September 3rd, 1783

2624. Which present-day states did the United States gain from France in the Louisiana Purchase on April 30th, 1803?
Arkansas, Missouri, Iowa, Oklahoma, Kansas, Nebraska, Minnesota, Texas, Montana, North Dakota, South Dakota, Colorado, Wyoming, New Mexico, and Louisiana

2625. During which years did the Lewis and Clark Expedition happen?
1804 – 1806

2626. What was the goal of the Lewis and Clark Expedition?
Exploring the western part of the United States

2627. What were the results of the Lewis and Clark Expedition?
Many maps of the United States about the Pacific Northwest region; the discovery of more than 200 new species of animals

2628. Which states did the Oregon Trail pass through?
Missouri, Iowa, Kansas, Nebraska, Colorado, Wyoming, Utah, Idaho, and Oregon

2629. What states did the Mormon Trail pass through?
Illinois, Iowa, Nebraska, Wyoming, and Utah

2630. In what year did the Mexican-American War start?
1846

2631. When was the Treaty of Guadalupe Hidalgo signed to end the Mexican-American War, and it granted most of Arizona (north of the Gila River) to the United States?
February 2th, 1848

2632. What was the Pony Express that existed during April 3rd, 1860 – October 1861?
A fast mail service carried by horseback riders from St. Joseph of Missouri to Sacramento of California

2633. Prior to the Civil War, which line separated the free states and the slave states of the United States?
Mason-Dixon Line

2634. The Mason-Dixon Line is based on the border of which two states?
Pennsylvania and Maryland

2635. When did the American Civil War begin?
April 12th, 1861

2636. Which states seceded from the United States during the Civil War?
South Carolina, Mississippi, Alabama, Florida, Georgia, Louisiana, Texas, Arkansas, North Carolina, Tennessee, and Virginia

2637. What was the new country consisting of the seceded states called?
Confederate States of America

2638. What was the first capital of the Confederate States of America?
Montgomery, Alabama

2639. What was the second capital of the Confederate States of America?
Richmond, Virginia

2640. What was the third and final capital of the Confederate States of America?

Danville, Virginia

2641. When did the American Civil War end?
April 9th, 1865

2642. What war did the United States fight during 1917 – 1918?
World War I

2643. Which countries did the United States ally with during World War I?
United Kingdom, Romania, Greece, Serbia, Belgium, France, Italy, and Japan

2644. Which countries did the United States fight against during World War I?
Germany, Austria-Hungary, Ottoman Empire, and Bulgaria

2645. What was the last war where the United States officially declared war (as of 2014)?
World War II

2646. During which period did the United States fight World War II?
December 8th, 1941 – September 2nd, 1945

2647. Which major countries did the United States ally with in World War II?
Soviet Union, China, and the United Kingdom

2648. Which major countries did the United States fight against in World War II?
Germany, Italy, and Japan

2649. During which years did the United States ally with the South Koreans in the Korean War?
1950 – 1953

2650. During which years did the United States intervene in Vietnam against Communist Vietnam?
1955 – 1975

2651. During which years did the United States fight the First Gulf War in Iraq?
1990 – 1991

2652. During which years did the United States invade Afghanistan?
2001 – Present

2653. During which years did the United States invade Iraq in the Iraq War?
2003 – 2011

Bibliography

- 50states.com, http://www.50states.com/
- Alaska Tour and Travel, http://www.alaskatravel.com/
- Answers.com - Online Dictionary, Encyclopedia and much more, http://www.answers.com/
- Background Notes, http://www.state.gov/r/pa/ei/bgn/
- Canada's Aquatic Environments, http://www.aquatic.uoguelph.ca/
- CIA – The World Factbook, https://www.cia.gov/library/publications/the-world-factbook/
- Enchanted Learning, http://www.enchantedlearning.com/usa/
- Free World Maps, http://www.freeworldmaps.net/united-states/
- Geography Page, http://peakbagger.com/
- Geography Summaries Index - Vaughn's Summaries, http://www.vaughns-1-pagers.com/geography/
- Infoplease: Encyclopedia, Almanac, Atlas, Biographies, Dictionary, Thesaurus. Free online reference, research & homework help, http://www.infoplease.com/
- Netstate.com, http://www.netstate.com/
- Official global voting platform of New7Wonders, http://www.new7wonders.com/
- Perry-Castañeda Map Collection - UT Library Online, http://lib.utexas.edu/maps/americas.html
- Visit USA, http://www.visitusa.com/
- Wikipedia – The Free Encyclopedia, http://en.wikipedia.org/wiki/Main_Page
- Wildlife National Parks & Wildlife Sanctuaries of the world, http://www.world-wildlife-adventures.com/
- World Atlas of Maps Flags and Geography Facts and Figures, http://www.worldatlas.com/
- World Database on Protected Areas, http://www.wdpa.org/
- World's Longest Rivers, http://rivers.wonderworld.us/
- World StateMen.org, http://www.worldstatesmen.org/
- World Travel, http://travel.mapsofworld.com/
- Wright Realtors, http://www.wrightrealtors.com/links/timeline/

Other Books

- World Geography Questionnaires: Americas – Countries and Territories in the Region (Volume 1), Kenneth Ma and Jennifer Fu, ISBN-10: 1449553222, ISBN-13: 978-1449553227
- World Geography Questionnaires: Africa – Countries and Territories in the Region (Volume 2), Kenneth Ma and Jennifer Fu, ISBN-10: 1451587074, ISBN-13: 978-1451587074
- World Geography Questionnaires: Oceania & Antarctica – Countries and Territories in the Region (Volume 3), Kenneth Ma and Jennifer Fu, ISBN-10: 1453665250, ISBN-13: 978-1453665251
- World Geography Questionnaires: Asia – Countries and Territories in the Region (Volume 4), Kenneth Ma and Jennifer Fu, ISBN-10: 1453831983, ISBN-13: 978-1453831984
- World Geography Questionnaires: Europe – Countries and Territories in the Region (Volume 5), Kenneth Ma and Jennifer Fu, ISBN-10: 1453833498, ISBN-13: 978-1453833490
- World Geography Terms – Human Geography and Physical Geography (Volume 6), Kenneth Ma and Jennifer Fu, ISBN-10: 1466329068, ISBN-13: 978-1466329065
- The Missing Mau, Hermione Ma and Jennifer Fu, ISBN-10: 1451587090, ISBN-13: 978-1451587098
- The Crazy College, Hermione Ma and Jennifer Fu, ISBN-10: 1452851174, ISBN-13: 978-1452851174
- The Revolving Resort, Hermione Ma and Jennifer Fu, ISBN-10: 1453815139, ISBN-13: 978-1453815137
- The Gingerbread Museum of Candy, Omelets, Spinach, Ice, and Biscuits, Hermione Ma, ISBN-10: 1477543252, ISBN-13: 978-1477543252
- ACE Your Java Interview, Jennifer Fu, ISBN-10: 1484104935, ISBN-13: 978-1484104934
- Bubble, Jennifer Fu, ISBN-10: 1461029120, ISBN-13: 978-1461029120

About the Authors

Kenneth Ma is a freshman in UC Davis. He was the National Geography School Bee at Eaton Elementary School in Cupertino when he was in fourth grade, and he was the National Geography School Bee at Kennedy Middle School in Cupertino when he was in sixth grade. He was also a member of the Kennedy Middle School National Geography Challenge Championship team in 2007. In 2007, he was honored with the Outstanding Achievement in Geography Award from his middle school. Besides his interest in Geography, Kenneth is also an avid soccer player.

Jennifer Fu is Kenneth's mom and lives in Cupertino, California. She is a software engineer by day and an aspiring writer by night. She has contributed short stories and novellas to a number of on-line publications in Chinese. Writing a geography book is a new endeavor for her.

Made in the USA
San Bernardino, CA
16 December 2016